PRAISE F

Bold Parents, Po

"Smart Christian parents will read Karen Dockrey's book *Bold Parents, Positive Teens.* It's practical, insightful, and informative."

> —DR. KEVIN LEMAN, author of *Making Children Mind Without Losing Yours*

"Karen Dockrey instills confidence in the *position* in which God has placed us as parents while enhancing our *performance* through hundreds of practical, daily-applicable suggestions."

> —DEAN AND PATTI ORRICO, parents of contemporary Christian music artist Stacie Orrico

"Karen's easy-to-follow action steps combine with deep insights into the inner workings of the teen mind. Best of all, she gives parents permission to step up to the challenge with faith, love, and confidence."

> —CARLA BARNHILL, editor of *Christian Parenting Today* magazine

"Teenagers can make good choices and live God-honoring lives, but they need parents who set limits and provide clear guidance. This book offers lots of ideas and practical examples for bringing out the best in our kids."

> —WAYNE RICE, cofounder of Youth Specialties and director of the Understanding Your Teenager seminars

"Karen Dockrey provides a wealth of specific applications and believable family dialogue. This book needs to be on your short list."

—RICHARD ROSS, PH.D., spokesperson for True Love Waits and coauthor of *30 Days: Turning the Hearts of Parents and Teenagers Toward Each Other*

"Karen Dockrey deals with the everyday stuff head-on, offering practical tools and examples. This book provides hope!"

—PAUL LARUE, father of Philip and Natalie LaRue of the Christian recording group LaRue

"*Bold Parents, Positive Teens* is a toolbox full of practical, biblical wisdom for parents. This is a fun, energizing read."

—TED HAGGARD, pastor and author of *The Life Giving Church* and *Letters from Home*

BOLD PARENTS, POSITIVE TEENS

LOVING AND GUIDING YOUR CHILD THROUGH

THE CHALLENGES OF ADOLESCENCE

BOLD PARENTS, POSITIVE TEENS

KAREN DOCKREY

WATERBROOK
PRESS

BOLD PARENTS, POSITIVE TEENS
PUBLISHED BY WATERBROOK PRESS
2375 Telstar Drive, Suite 160
Colorado Springs, Colorado 80920
A division of Random House, Inc.

Scripture taken from the *Holy Bible, New International Version*®. NIV®. Copyright © 1973, 1978, 1984 by International Bible Society. Used by permission of Zondervan Publishing House. All rights reserved.

Details in some anecdotes and stories have been changed to protect the identities of the persons involved.

ISBN 1-57856-493-X

Library of Congress Cataloging-in-Publication Data

Dockrey, Karen, 1955–
  Bold parents, positive teens : loving and guiding your child through the challenges of adolescence / Karen Dockrey.— 1st ed.
     p. cm.
  ISBN 1-57856-493-X
  1. Parenting—Religious aspects—Christianity. 2. Parent and teenager—Religious aspects— Christianity. I. Title.
  BV4529 .D635 2002
  248.8'45—dc21
                              2002008733

Printed in the United States of America
2002—First Edition

10 9 8 7 6 5 4 3 2 1

CONTENTS

DON'T BELIEVE THE RUMORS

You know the sound of "Daaad!" And "Mo-*ther!*" These are clear signs that adolescence has arrived. Your teenager begins to question what you say rather than trust you as the smartest person in the universe. He now prefers that you become invisible in public places, blending into the background Secret Service–style, rather than be seen with him.

This is a difficult and confusing time for parents who wonder if they've lost all the fun and closeness they used to share with their kids. But happily, the good days are far from over. Adolescence marks the beginning of a fresh adventure, not an ever deepening doom. Don't believe the rumors that tell you teenagers are people to dread. Every single day, all over the world, real teenagers remain close to real parents. Every day real parents equip their teenagers to journey successfully toward independent adulthood. Every day real teenagers communicate with their parents about what is deep in their minds and heavy on their hearts. Every day parents and teens work together to accomplish God's purposes. It's an intense but first-class process of growing to maturity that is led by our very good God. With God guiding the process, you have real reason for optimism.

NEW MONSTERS TO CHASE AWAY

But wait a minute! If every day real teenagers stay close to real parents, why do so many parents spend so much time fighting with their teens?

Why do so many teenagers pull away from their parents? It's because there are fire-breathing monsters out there eager to consume your teenagers. These monsters include lack of communication, bad friends, self-centeredness, irresponsibility, disobedience, temptations, destructive patterns, and lack of spiritual connection. But that's not all. There is also laziness (on the part of teens *or* parents), unharnessed emotions, and outright rebellion. You can't chase these monsters away with a flashlight as you could when your kids were toddlers. But you can tame them just as effectively. This book will show you how.

THE FEAR MONSTER

To prepare for monster slaying, you need to know a few facts about the monsters your teens grapple with. For one thing, these enemies use a new weapon against parents, the weapon of fear. There's a lot to be afraid of when you're parenting teens.

- What if your teenagers stop talking to you and you lose the closeness you've built all these years?
- What if your teenagers fall in with the wrong crowd and mess up their entire lives with a few dumb choices?
- What if, when you discipline your teenagers, they rebel and never come back?
- What if your teenagers question God and then reject their faith?
- What if your teenagers never develop the life skills they need to become responsible, independent adults?

These aren't irrational fears since these things can and do happen to teenagers every day. What doesn't make sense is to sit idly by and wait. Though you've heard it a billion times, it's simply not true that "once kids enter the teen years, there's nothing parents can do." Nor is it true that if you pray and leave it all up to God, things will turn out all right.

Godly success requires action. Every day, parents and teens work together to fight off the monsters that threaten them, their relationships, and their God-given purposes. You must take initiative, like the father portrayed in Luke 15. In this parable, the father represents God, who not only waits patiently for us to return to him, but who also constantly watches for us and runs to embrace us, drawing us close to him.

When God says not to worry in verses such as Matthew 6:25-34, he specifies certain things not to worry about. These are life circumstances that are beyond our control, such as how long we'll live (see verse 27). Other matters we do control. So rather than do nothing, this passage teaches us to turn our worries into effective action. God shows us how to do this as he directs us to seek his kingdom and his righteousness (see verse 33).

God knows what our teenagers need. So talk with him first, and keep conversing so he can show you just when to talk and when to keep silent, when to show how and when to let your teen try for herself, when to discipline and when to show mercy, when to offer a strategy and when to enforce that strategy. In so doing you'll fulfill your God-given responsibility to guide your teens through the minefields of adolescence, from dependence to responsible independence.

Every day God guides parents to prevent tragedies in their teens' lives, such as bad friends, dumb choices, destructive rebellion, faith rejection, and ingrained irresponsibility. He shows parents how to turn their teens around once they have started down a bad path. And in the process, real teenagers and real parents enjoy mastering life together. So put on your armor, pick up your sword, and get ready to do some monster slaying. Then live free of fear with your teenage princess or prince.

THE SELFISHNESS MONSTER

Once you overcome worry and fear by seeking God's guidance in parenting your teens, the monsters will breathe another type of fire in your direction: selfishness. Good parenting takes tons of work and requires exhausting intensity: It isn't for cowards, and it's not for the selfish.

It takes firmness to tell a teen, "No, you won't do this," or, "Yes, you will do this," and then put up with his relentless complaining over how unfair you are. It's much easier to exclaim, "All right, just do what you want!"

It takes energy to stay home from your job or evening event to make certain your teen doesn't go ahead and do what you prohibited. It's much easier to claim, "Well, I can't supervise her all the time. I'm just going to have to trust her."

It takes persistence to keep saying no to dangerous behaviors and to motivate your teen to choose the good behaviors instead. It's much easier to say, "Well, if he's bent on destroying his life, I can't stop him."

It takes firmness to make your teens speak respectfully to you and to insist that they treat their siblings like valuable people. It's much easier to say, "All families fight."

But as you choose to quench this fire with everything you have and without giving in, the complaining will eventually yield to trusting your advice. Your extra supervision will give way to your teen choosing to embrace the how and why of the rules. Your tireless motivation will give way to the ecstasy of watching your teen choose well for himself. Your insistence that siblings be treated with kindness will give way to a lifetime of family closeness and support.

Too many parents focus on their own feelings, interests, or plans instead of investing the needed energy in parenting. Too many parents are too self-centered, often without even realizing it, to make the temporary sacrifices that will produce the family life God wants us to enjoy. You and I will become these same selfish parents if we don't consistently and continually choose otherwise. So overcome your selfishness, buck up against your fears, and keep on doing what is right, even when it's difficult and even when you don't feel like it.

REASONS FOR CONFIDENCE

Many parenting books characterize teens as impossible to deal with, urging you to simply make it through these dark days and hope that somehow your teenagers will turn out all right. Other books urge you to focus on understanding your teens' emotional and spiritual needs, being careful not to interfere and make things worse for them. Such viewpoints see the complexity of adolescence as "no parents' land," a place where teens must figure out how to make it on their own. Those books warn that if parents get too involved, teens will rebel and never come back to the fold. This advice is not only harmful to teenagers; it instills fear and insecurity in the hearts of parents.

It's time for a new approach that gives parents credit for their wisdom and builds their confidence so they can become the godly parents their teenagers really need. The teen years are not the time to back down; the teen years are the time to step up your efforts. If you refuse to actively parent your teens, the ten monsters of the teenage years, which we will look at in the following chapters, will consume both you and your kids. If you back down during these years, your teenagers will establish patterns of unhappiness that will persist into their futures and into the lives of their own children.

However, when you choose to actively parent your teenagers, you'll armor them against attacks and equip them to build castles of happiness. The influence you possess is enormous, and the God-given good that you can do will carry over into future generations.

This book won't give you every answer—only God knows exactly what your family needs at just this moment. But it will show you ten God-guided principles you can implement to armor yourself and your teenagers against the monsters that threaten to disrupt your family and steal your happiness. By choosing a few courageous actions now, you can gather in God's kingdom and enjoy the feasts of life. Your teenagers and your God are counting on you.

MY TEENAGER WON'T

TALK TO ME

HELP YOUR TEEN EXPRESS AND HEAR THOUGHTS, FEELINGS, AND DREAMS

"How did things go at school today?"

"Fine."

"Anything new happen?"

"Nope."

"What are you planning for this weekend?"

"Oh, nothing much."

Sound familiar? Your precious teenager returns home, and you long to share in her life. But all you get in answer to your questions are single-syllable responses expressed in a monotone. How can you shift your conversations from vague generalities to actual thoughts, feelings, goals, and dreams?

First, reject the myth that noncommunication is normal for teenagers. You've heard it said over and over: "Teenagers just don't talk to their parents. You'll have to accept the fact that they clam up and hole up in their rooms." It may be common for teens to avoid talking to you, but it's not normal. Teenagers long for a caring adult to hear and understand their thoughts, dreams, and ideas. If that person is a family member, the connection is all the more treasured. Why? Because such a listener invests in the teen's life on a daily basis and genuinely cares about what happens to her. Even better, the interest is lifelong.

Now, let's dismiss a second myth, that talking isn't that big of a deal. The truth is that talking is crucial. Good communication is the foundation for every life skill: work, friendship, learning, marriage, expressing our faith, and all of our decisions and feelings. So invest regularly in talking with your teen. She desperately needs this connection with her parents so she can navigate the choppy waters of adolescence. She needs you to help her sort out ideas, feelings, and dreams. Take every opportunity to show her how.

If you don't know how to communicate, now is the time to learn. Because we weren't born knowing how to be parents, we each must learn how to teach and guide our teenagers to communicate effectively. This matters greatly, because your teen is trying to find answers that will shape her future. Teenagers wrestle with weighty questions: "Is God real?" "Why do I feel this way?" "Do I have any power over what happens or what doesn't happen?" "Which way should I go?" "Does God even care?"

All of these life questions, and all life decisions, find solutions through good communication. But your teen won't ever ask the questions aloud if you don't show her how. Take this opportunity to dismiss another myth, the one that says talking should come naturally. No one is born with excellent communication abilities. Good communication is a *learned* skill. During the roller-coaster years of adolescence, feelings and experiences become so intense that even the chattiest kids find things hard to put into words. A decision to simply stop talking or to rely on the communication skills of the youth workers at church is not the solution. Instead you must teach your teens how to talk and how to listen. You are the person God has put in place to guide this critical process. So be deliberate about it.

If our teenagers practice communication skills through the throes of adolescence, they will know how to talk and listen through tough times that come later in life. If we fail to teach them these skills, our teens will flounder both now and later as adults. In lonely desperation they will turn to others who will give bad advice or no advice at all. Our teens will be tossed about rather than find security in home, in family, and in God. Scary? You betcha.

So be intentional about setting aside your qualms and taking effective action. You can choose to learn what you don't already know about communication and then decisively teach your teen. Start with what you do know: You know what it means to be heard, understood, and disagreed with respectfully. You also know what it means to be guided well, without the extremes of dictatorship and spinelessness. So provide those good experiences for your teens. Refuse to make them feel stupid as you teach them. Instead, steadily supply the know-how and the practice to make them caring communicators.

SHOW THEM HOW

When teaching any skill, begin with something that is doable to build confidence. To help your teens develop their communication skills, start by implementing a say-three-things-a-day rule. This worked well, although gradually, with Ellie, who had never been chatty as a child. As she entered the agonizing years of middle school, she became even quieter, dangerously so. One day after school, her mom said, "Ellie, I know we don't usually talk much, but because we're family I'd like us to change that. Every day I'm going to tell you about three things that happened to me and how I feel about them. And I want you to tell me three things you're thinking or feeling or experiencing. I will listen carefully to everything you tell me, and I hope you'll listen back."

"Oh, Mom!" Ellie rolled her eyes and kept reading her magazine.

"I'm serious, Ellie. We'll start at supper tonight."

"Whatever," Ellie mumbled.

This wasn't the first time Ellie's mom had tried to start something new. So Ellie figured this one would last about as long as the others—a day or two—and then her mom would forget all about this new emphasis on talking.

That evening, after saying a blessing over dinner, her mom introduced the plan for family conversation. "We'll take turns telling three things about our day. Do you want to go first, Ellie?"

"Um, okay. Whatever. Math class was boring."

That wasn't exactly what Ellie's parents had in mind, but her dad decided to follow the same line of thought. "I had to sit through a boring meeting at work today," he told the others.

"I was bored sitting in traffic on the way home," her mom added.

"I wasn't bored at school, because we had a speaker," said Ellie's younger brother, Ethan.

"Who was your speaker?" his mom asked.

"Some guy who had been in a car accident because of drinking and now is in a wheelchair," Ethan said. "He told us never to drink and drive. But I'm too young to drink anyway."

"Not drinking is a good habit to start now," his dad said, "long before you get your license."

"What else happened today, Ellie?" her mom asked.

"Nothing. Just school."

Her mom kept asking questions, so Ellie volunteered two more nonevents just to get it over with. Then she asked to be excused.

Ten-year-old Ethan chatted away. "Can I tell more than three things?"

IT'LL TAKE TIME

After the kids left the dinner table, Ellie's parents assessed their experiment.

"Well, that went well!" whispered Ellie's dad with mock seriousness.

"I don't know if that was good or not, but we agreed that we'd try this for a month, and we have twenty-nine more days to get it right."

The next night only Ellie and her mom were home. Her dad was working late, and Ethan had ball practice. Ellie assumed that meant she was off the hook.

"So what three things do you want to talk about today, Ellie?" her mom asked while they put supper on the table.

"You go first, Mom," Ellie suggested, eager to get this pretend closeness over with.

TOP TALK STARTERS

Most kids don't relish the idea of coming home and having to relive the details of a stressful day. So when you try to get them to open up, move past "What did you learn in school?" Instead, try some of these:

"What was the best and worst thing about your day?"

"What good thing did God poke into your day today?"

"What's happening in that book you've been reading?" (Or ask a similar question related to what your teen enjoys most.)

"Your friends were happy to see you when I dropped you off at school. How did things go today?"

"You've been doing really well this week controlling your temper. What's your secret?"

"Thanks for helping with the dishes last night." (Appreciation invites comfort in talking.)

"What frustrated you the most about this day?"

"You look happy! What good thing brought that smile?"

"Wanna tell me about it?" Then wait...and wait...and continue to keep quiet and stay close by so your teen knows you really want to hear.

"You were hoping to talk to that one guy at school. How's that been going?"

"Well, I think I made a new client happy. He was cantankerous, but I kept answering back calmly."

"I didn't do that so well," Ellie said before she realized she was volunteering a feeling. "Margo was crabby, and I snapped at her."

"What happened then?"

"She snapped right back. 'Well, aren't you in a mood!' she said. Then I said, 'Well, I was in a good mood until I ran into you!'"

"Then what?" asked Ellie's mom, continuing to pull together supper preparations so she wouldn't look too interested.

"Well, she didn't say a word to me the rest of the day."

"Bummer."

"Yeah," said Ellie. "Now I don't know what to do."

"This is a rough one," her mom acknowledged.

"Yep," Ellie said. "I don't really want to talk about it."

"I can understand. It's pretty painful."

"Yep," said Ellie.

This is where things got tricky. Ellie's mom had an urge to provide a solution to her daughter's problem. Ellie could apologize to Margo—maybe send her an e-mail or call her. Or she could wait until the next day to see how things went when she saw Margo at school. Ellie's mom wanted to express these suggestions and more, but she held her tongue. She realized that giving too much advice could cause her daughter to clam up. So she stayed quiet and focused on listening. The conversation moved to safer topics: whether Ellie wanted mild or hot taco sauce, how many taco shells she wanted, if she would chop the onions.

Finally tears welled up in Ellie's eyes. "What am I going to do, Mom?"

"Well, maybe just go to Margo and tell her what you're feeling. Say that you're sad about the way you treated her."

"She'll think I'm dumb if I say that," argued Ellie. "She'd just call me sappy."

HOW TO SILENCE EVEN THE MOST TALKATIVE TEEN

Teenagers stop talking not because they don't want to express themselves but because they get flamed when they try. There's never a good
time to make your teenager feel dumb. This doesn't mean you always
agree with her, but it does mean that you disagree with respect for the
irreplaceable person your teen is.

If you resort to any of the following statements, you will muzzle
your teen.

- "That's a stupid idea!" Just because you would do it differently, that
  doesn't mean your teen is wrong. Whether your teen is wrong or
  right, encourage further thinking with, "Tell me more about why
  you think your idea will work. What are the advantages and dis-
  advantages of that plan?"
- "Why can't you be like your brother?" Your teen has strengths
  that his sibling doesn't have and vice versa. If you're frustrated with
  a certain behavior, deal with it directly. Don't compare him to
  someone else.
- "That is so typical!" There's a thing called self-fulfilling prophecy,
  and low expectations are not the way to use it. When you assume
  your teen will fail at whatever she is attempting, she will make
  good on your lack of confidence by failing.
- "How could you *do* a thing like that?" Accusations get in the way
  of solving the problem. Instead of accusing, move your teen—and
  yourself—from bad feelings to right actions. Once your teen gets
  into a mess, show him the steps to take to repair any damage
  and to make better choices in the future. Share the fact that
  everybody makes mistakes, even you. Continue by insisting that
  he actually clean up the mess he has made. Follow through; don't
  just talk.

"Maybe. Or she might really appreciate it. A good apology takes the fuel out of a fight."

"Oh, Mom, you just don't understand! People don't do stuff like that at my school."

Her mom wanted to argue back, to say that apologies are always a good beginning. She wanted to suggest more solutions. She had a strong urge to prove her point. But instead she offered, "What do you think might work?"

"I don't know, Mom. I just don't know. Maybe I could write her a note."

"Sometimes notes take the strong emotions out of a conversation. But notes can also get passed to everyone in the school," her mom cautioned.

"I don't know what to do!" Ellie cried.

Ellie's mom wanted to say that the two girls could work things out, just as they had done in the past. But Ellie was despairing. To gloss it over would trivialize her feelings. So she avoided giving more advice. Instead, she asked, "Anything else come to mind?"

"I just want to let it blow over," Ellie said. "Anything to keep Margo from being mad at me."

"I hate it when someone's mad at me," Ellie's mom responded, trying to affirm the feeling behind her daughter's words.

NOTICE THE RESULTS

Ellie continued to worry that night about her flareup with Margo, but the following day she came home in a cheerful mood. Her mom was thrilled but tried to play it cool.

"Wow, your day must have gone well! What happened?"

"Well, I told Margo I was sad about the things I said yesterday. She had looked like she wanted to fight when I walked up to her, but then, when I apologized, her expression changed, and she said she was sad too. We walked to class like nothing bad had happened between us."

"I'm impressed," said Ellie's mom.

"Me, too. I didn't want to write a note to her because everyone can read those. But I was really scared to say something out loud," Ellie explained. "Then somehow seeing Margo made it easier."

WHAT IF MY TEEN RESISTS TALKING?

Some teenagers are destined to be trial attorneys. No matter what technique a parent tries, the teen has a reason he can't talk about it.

If your teen says, "You'll never understand!" you can respond with "Try me. I know I haven't always understood in the past, but try me this time." (GOAL: Affirm that your teen's feelings, dreams, or disappointments really are important.)

If your teen says, "I don't want to talk about it," you can respond with "We're family, so we help each other. Tell me at least two things, and I'll let you off the hook. Then later we'll talk a bit more until we solve it together." (GOAL: Demonstrate that your teen never has to face life alone.)

If your teen says, "You'll think it's dumb," you can respond with "If it's important to you, it's important to me." (GOAL: Demonstrate that no problem is too small to take seriously.)

If your teen says, "This is *my* room. You can't just barge in here!" you can respond with "I always knock first. Anyway, we're family and we don't hide anything." (GOAL: Communicate that privacy does not give license to hide wrong possessions or plans.)

If your teen doesn't offer an excuse but simply refuses to talk, you can respond with "You can go out with your friends after you tell me three things for three days in a row. If you remain quiet, though, you'll have to stay home with me this weekend." (GOAL: Show that communicating with parents earns privileges.)

"I'm so glad," her mom said.

"Me, too," said Ellie as she ducked her head into the refrigerator. "Are we out of sharp cheddar again? I was hoping for a sandwich."

Ellie's mom was glad her daughter couldn't see her jaw drop in realization that Ellie had listened to her idea and adopted it as her own. She decided to let Ellie think it was her own idea. After all, the goal of advice is to get our teens to think well for themselves.

TWO STEPS BACKWARD

A few days later Ellie was sullen again. The family was eating supper late, which meant everyone was tired, but Ellie's parents were determined to keep the everybody-share process going.

Ethan had no problem, cheerfully chattering about that evening's church classes. But Ellie didn't want to talk.

TRANSLATE "LISTEN"

When our teens cry out, "Can't you just listen?" it seldom means "Just sit and look at me." It can mean a number of important things, such as:

- Will you let me talk first?
- Will you listen to me long enough to understand rather than assume you already know my feelings?
- Will you give me short answers rather than long lectures?
- Will you be quiet long enough for me to reach the conclusion that I've been wrong (or right) about this?
- Will you value what I've said even when you're talking?
- Will you show me how to handle this without making me look dumb?
- When you have to correct me, will you make it clear where God is still working through me?

"What's happening in your life, Ellie?" her dad asked, after Ethan shared all three of his details without missing a breath.

"Nothing," said Ellie.

"Come on. We really want to hear."

"I said 'nothing,' and that's what I meant!"

"She's mad because Ty was talking to another girl tonight," Ethan reported.

"Shut up, Ethan!" said Ellie just before she stormed out of the room.

"Ellie, you can't use 'shut up,'" her dad called after her. "And, Ethan, that's not your story to tell. Excuse yourself please, and go apologize to your sister."

"Can I come back and finish eating after I talk to Ellie?" Ethan fretted.

"We'll see. Your first priority is making things right with your sister," his dad insisted.

What happened to the relaxed conversation and natural give-and-take of a few days earlier? Time happened. Moods and events shift, making it easier to talk on one day, more difficult on the next. And the fewer the people, the more easily conversation flows.

So should you talk only on the easy-to-talk days or only when there are two of you?

Nope.

Those times come too seldom. And you miss the benefit of full-family closeness if you choose only two-person conversations. As tempting as it is to let sleeping squabbles lie, find ways to solve tense situations. Establish the following talking rules that every family member must practice, in both good times and bad:

- "That's not your story to tell" means that nobody tells anyone else's story or experience.
- "What you say matters to me" means that everyone listens carefully to every story.

- "You talk. Then you listen" means we take turns, so no one can dominate the conversation.
- "Tell what you liked about what I just said" means that everyone will comment positively on each other's ideas rather than focus only on their own.
- "Laugh lovingly" means when I laugh, it's to make you feel smart and witty, not stupid or foolish.
- "Care on purpose" means no matter how cross or tired I am, I will intentionally treat you with kindness.

Just as important as establishing these talking rules is enforcing them. You really can legislate morality long enough to show how and why moral action works for everyone's benefit. You don't let your toddlers eat candy for meals just because they don't have a commitment to good eating. You feed them the food that will nourish them,

---

HOW TO JUMP-START TALKING FOR EVEN THE MOST RELUCTANT TEEN

Use praise. Few teenagers can resist a genuine compliment. You may get eye rolling, but inside they'll like it. So every day tell your teens something different that you like about them. Include personality characteristics, wise choices, and appearance. After a while your teens will trust you enough to tell you a tidbit or two.

Be present. Be available at the time when your teens process the stuff of the day. For many, this is right after school or when they get home from sports and other after-school activities. Consider picking up your nondriving teen so you'll have uninterrupted time to listen. Or stop what you're doing when he walks in the door. If you're at work, call daily at the time your teen arrives home, or have your teen call you at this time. This habit gives regular opportunities to connect.

---

even if they demonstrate a strong preference for sweets. In the same way, Ellie's parents don't let their son and daughter say whatever they want just because siblings are prone to do that.

When Ethan is certain he'll get in trouble for invading his sister's privacy, he'll stop doing it. But if his parents allowed him to pick on his sister, Ellie would one-up him by telling stuff about him. Then he'd get back at her by telling one of her secrets that he swore he wouldn't tell. And she'd privately use that one word guaranteed to make him explode and kick the wall. On and on the bickering would go until their relationship would no longer hold any trust or affection. To avoid this too-frequent outcome, their parents work hard at stopping the sibling compulsion to get-her-worse-than-she-got-me. The solution to this natural tendency, according to the Bible, is turning the other cheek (see Matthew 5:39). This surprise action will put an end to escalating retaliation.

Prompt but don't pry. Ask open-ended questions: "What did you like about that?" "How do you think they'll act next?" "If you could do it over again, how would you change things?" Use your questions to invite conversations rather than pry. (If your teen claims that *all* questions pry, you can lightheartedly reply, "Well, prying is what parents do best!")

Be predictable. Establish talking time that your teen can count on. For Ellie's family it's the tradition of telling three things at supper. For you it might be working on a jigsaw puzzle every weekend, or just-you-and-me talking time during the regular drive to soccer practice.

Don't pounce. Pick up tidbits carefully so your teen won't withdraw. Your teen will test you by sharing simple stuff before sharing the deep stuff. So when he says he saw a duck on the way home from gymnastics, show that you're interested. Even if he's teasing you, go ahead and ask: "What was the duck doing?"

And don't forget that, as parents, you have to obey the rules right along with your children. As each family member avidly listens and genuinely treasures what the other person has to say, each one will want to tell more. Few things build communication faster than knowing that other people care about what you have to say.

Then a Step Forward

Ellie's mom could hardly wait to see her daughter the next day after school. Maybe Ellie would talk about whatever had been bothering her the night before.

"Hi, honey, I'm glad you're home," she said as Ellie walked into the house.

"Hi, Mom," said Ellie. Her mom couldn't tell if she'd had an easy day or a rough one.

"What happened today that was really good?" she ventured.

"Not much."

No amount of prompting would get Ellie to talk, and her mom knew better than to try to force anything at this time. But a few days later, Ellie was full of news.

"Coach R. liked my English presentation. I didn't go first like you always tell me to. But I did go third. That's soon enough that he can't compare me to the whole class."

"I'm so happy he liked it," her mom said. "You've been working really hard on that presentation."

"No kidding," said Ellie. "I'm really glad it's over."

"And that it went well," said Mom.

"Exactly."

There were lots of details at first, then less as Ellie finished the story. But this is plenty of interchange for one conversation. Ellie's mom still hadn't heard what happened with Ty the week before, but she could wait. The two were sharing life. Other things were on Ellie's mind right now.

The process of learning the life skills we need to succeed as adults and the relational skills that honor God begins with good communication. Over time, Ellie's mom taught her daughter not only how to share her own life, but also how to listen carefully to others. Teenagers need to hear as well as speak. They also need to receive wisdom when their parents have something to pass on. This is the give and take of conversation, of family, of learning, and of the good life.

TALKING TO YOUR OWN TEENAGER

The story about Ellie and her parents is somewhat typical, but teens differ just as parents do. Your teenager won't follow the time line Ellie followed. Your teen may talk more or less, argue more or less, and cooperate better or not as well. But don't give up. Keep teaching your teen to talk and to listen. Keep learning to communicate better yourself. Keep trying different connection strategies until you find the balance that works for your one-of-a-kind family.

The time line with your son or daughter won't be the same, but two things are true of all teenagers: (1) No matter how much your teen claims otherwise, she wants caring communication with you. (2) Your teenager also wants to know what you think and why. You can confidently move forward based on these characteristics of all teenagers.

Don't give up on working toward better and better communication. It takes perseverance, and you'll experience occasional setbacks. But remember, good communication is the basis for all the life skills your teen needs to learn.

TO INVITE TALKING

Sitting down to just talk can be too intense or awkward. So add a comfort cushion like these:

- *Chaperone the group.* Your teen and his friends will talk as if you're invisible while you drive the car.
- *Work on a project together.* The chores of life are good places to connect. Rebuild an engine, sew a dress, work a puzzle, bake a casserole, or make dinner together. The task at hand absorbs nervous energy so you can give calmness to conversation. Doing this daily leads to your teen saving her news for this time she can count on.
- *Let your teen have friends over.* There's a certain safety in numbers, and your teen may say in a group what he won't say one-on-one. Let the gatherings be those you walk in and out of. Refuse to let the kids hole up in the basement or another room out of earshot. You're not eavesdropping as much as you're providing good supervision.
- *Take a walk.* Walking together avoids too-close-for-comfort eye contact but gives the privacy for opening up. A regular habit of walking and listening lets your teen know she can save up things to tell you and that there will be a reliable time to talk.
- *Use car time.* Talk during the time en route to a place you usually go, such as school or church or the grocery store. Or go to a place especially for conversation, such as a restaurant or a favorite talking spot.
- *Use a look of ultimate love.* When you invite your teen to talk, include a no-matter-what look of unconditional love. Even if your teen says nothing, you will have made a connection.

ACTION STEPS

Even when things are tense or emotional, show your teenager how to connect and reconnect with you. Whatever your communication style, use it to teach your teenager how to talk with you and with other family members.

- If you tease well, use that: "Ellie, you had two boys cornered at church this morning. That's a pretty creative way to get them talking to you."
- If you tell stories, use that: "Let me tell you about how well Ellie welcomed her guests during her party last week. First she…"
- If you spar, spar positively: "C'mon, Ethan, tell me even more ways you triumphed over math."

No matter what style you use, craft each word deliberately to guide your family to Christlike interaction, firmly aware that you are first and foremost a teacher of how to live in a way that honors God.

What Scripture says: "Do not let any unwholesome talk come out of your mouths, but only what is helpful for building others up according to their needs" (Ephesians 4:29).

Explain to your teen: "Your thoughts, ideas, dreams, and questions matter. Because we're family, we want to walk alongside you. That happens as we talk and listen to each other."

[2]

I DON'T LIKE MY TEENAGER'S FRIENDS

GUIDE A WISER CHOICE IN COMPANIONS

Gregory has grown sullen and defensive. His parents trace his shift in attitude back to Haley, a neighborhood girl their son spends a lot of time with. Haley's parents aren't around much. They both work long hours, and after work they volunteer at church. They aren't deliberately neglectful, but they don't give Haley the supervision she needs. She goes wherever she wants whenever she wants.

Haley is talented and artistic, but she makes poor grades, criticizes anyone who tries to offer guidance, and wears clothing that sends the wrong signals. Though she became a Christian at last summer's teen Bible camp, she rejects churchgoers as hypocrites. Her parents pray for her, but they don't follow up their prayers with appropriate action. Quite simply, they have abdicated their God-given responsibility to guide their daughter each day.

Gregory can see that Haley is struggling. In fact, he was initially attracted to her because he wanted to connect her with the church youth group. And he did have a good influence on Haley for a while.

Then Haley started to influence Gregory. The effects were gradual, but his parents started noticing that his wardrobe was changing. He began wearing dark colors and T-shirts bearing antisocial slogans. Even

25

his language changed. His respect for God, for his teachers, and for his former friends slowly turned to defiance.

"Why do I need to go to church?" he asked his dad. "They're just a bunch of hypocrites who won't look past the way people are dressed."

Church wasn't the only problem. Gregory began to withdraw from his parents and from the activities he previously enjoyed. He began missing softball practices and eventually quit the team. When longtime friends called him, he turned down their invitations to go places. "They talk bad about Haley," he told his parents. "They just don't understand her."

"Maybe there's something to what they say," his dad suggested. "They've never been prone to gossip before."

"Well, they've changed. They're just as bad as the church bunch. They judge people rather than get to know people."

Gregory eventually dressed exclusively in extreme clothing. He threw away his Christian rock band T-shirts, favoring black outfits. He seldom smiled, and he became critical of anyone but Haley and her angry comrades. He claimed he was old enough to make his own choices, but the choices he made were exactly those Haley made. It wasn't long before Gregory's former friends stopped calling.

Haley was attractive and winsome, and it was clear that Gregory enjoyed the attention she gave him. Their relationship seemed platonic rather than romantic. Even so, Haley was bringing out more bad in Gregory than good.

Gregory's parents hoped that somehow their son would pull out of it. But Haley's influence over him became increasingly pervasive. Was there anything Gregory's parents could do, or is the choice of friends really a teenager's prerogative?

Yes, there is much parents can do. The teen years are the most critical time for parents to guide friendships. Your parenting is not over in this area. In many ways, it's just beginning.

SEE IT AS A TEACHING THING

Friends are more than the people your teen happens to spend time with. From his group of friends, your teenager will learn values, establish an identity, and eventually choose a life mate. Once Gregory starts running with a certain group, others will assume that he thinks and believes as that group does. Because he dresses in black, dyes his hair in wild colors, and wears spiked jewelry, others will assume he's an angry,

---

CHOICES THAT HELP

To help your teenager find friends who are worthy of the name, guide him to practice habits that help to express feelings, promote closeness, solve problems, develop confidence, and weave Christlikeness into life. Also, help your teen choose friends who practice these same habits. Here are the habits and their benefits:

- *Contentment.* Enjoys the simple things, is comfortable, enhances mutuality, provides the security to grow, brings out the good in others.
- *Honesty.* Reduces fear, protects a teen's reputation, promotes trust and closeness, deals directly with problems.
- *Kindness.* Enhances togetherness, endears friends to you, reduces a desire for revenge.
- *Talking calmly.* Harnesses anger, chips away at fears, avoids confusion, prevents resentment.
- *Being direct.* Halts game playing, lets each person know where the other stands, promotes the honest expression of needs and feelings.
- *Honoring God.* Provides a moral gauge for behavior: Would you say those things to Jesus? Would you choose that action with God watching? If so, proceed. If not, change your plans.

alienated person. This is not judgment, as Gregory claims; it's simply evaluation and discernment.

When Gregory discovers that people evaluate him based on dress and friendships, he may grow even angrier. But this anger will fade as he gains understanding of the hows and whys behind the reactions of others. Initially he will argue that no one stops to see beneath the surface. But people *are* seeing beneath the surface. The truth is, by choosing his friends Gregory has chosen an identity. By choosing his clothes, he has selected the messages he wants to send. What's on the surface works its way into his character. Gregory, like all teenagers, adopts actions that match his outward appearance.

God knew the powerful influence of those we associate with when he imposed strict limitations on whom the Israelites were to marry. The same phenomenon was active back then. People become like the people they spend time with. When the Israelites entered the Promised Land, God commanded them to drive out the former inhabitants. This sounds harsh, but God knew that intermingling with pagan nations would influence the children of Israel to forsake their God. Today, this is the reason we need regular times of fellowship with other believers. It is the reason our closest friendships must be with Christians. It's also the reason God requires Christians to marry only other practicing believers (see Deuteronomy 7:1-6; 2 Corinthians 6:14-17). This is not snobbery or elitism; it's recognizing reality. We become like those we spend time with.

Gregory, a teenager who initially practiced an active imitation of Christ, has begun to think like Haley. He is adopting her sense of meaninglessness and her combative attitude. Gregory's parents must show him how to ease out of this friendship and restore the healthy friendships he has started shunning. When a parent leaves a teenager to his own poor choices, others will take advantage of him. Gregory's parents must show him how to choose and build friendships with those who build his character rather than drain him of the good things he has to offer.

The good news is that parents can guide their teens' choice of friends in ways that neither invade privacy nor take away independence. Gregory's parents began by acknowledging his sincere interest in helping Haley connect more closely with God. His initial motives were pure. But that couldn't stop Haley's negative influence on him. She didn't consciously set out to pull Gregory away from good character or from sports and his friends. But she was so needy that she had little to give to Gregory or to anyone else. She had established patterns of taking from others, not giving and receiving in healthy balance. Because her parents failed to give her the nurture and instruction she needed, Haley drained Gregory dry and still demanded more. If he had been honest with himself, he would have admitted that he felt trapped—that he didn't know how to break loose from Haley's needy grip. But he felt guilty, and he didn't want to leave Haley in her hour of need.

Like all teenagers, Gregory and Haley need an assortment of people who love and care about them. Every teen needs a circle of healthy love, including that of friends, parents, and other caring adults. Haley is missing one of these factors—the involvement of parents. So she drains—rather than replenishes—those around her. Gregory's parents can't change Haley or her family situation, but they must change the circle of people who influence their son. In addition to his parents' love, Gregory needs a collection of healthy friends who are loved by their own parents.

Helping him switch allegiances from Haley and her circle of friends to a new set of friends will be a struggle. But it's entirely doable. Gregory's parents will make it happen by going slowly, by showing their son how to pull it off with care, and by making sure they include others in loving and caring for their son.

DEMONSTRATE THE PRINCIPLE

To help Gregory grasp the damaging effect of his friendship with Haley, his dad thought of an effective object lesson.

"Gregory, stand on this chair," his dad told him. "See, you are on a higher plane than me. You have high ideals, deep commitment, and determined values. You want very much to pull me up to your level of commitment.

"Let's say that I'm your age, and I go to church on Sundays. But

---

HOW TO PULL AWAY FROM A DESTRUCTIVE FRIENDSHIP

Suppose your teen can see that a friendship brings out the worst in him. Here are five suggestions you can give him for pulling away without hurting the troubled friend.

1. *Be busy.* When this friend calls or comes over, your teen can honestly say, "I wish I could spend time with you, but I have another commitment." (This "wish" is not a lie—your teen really does wish this friend was the kind of person he could spend time with.)

2. *Be together.* When your teenager does spend time with an unhealthy friend, make sure at least one other encouraging friend goes along. Then the two can band together to overcome the sometimes-negative influence of the troubled friend (see Ecclesiastes 4:12).

3. *Be brief.* Don't ask your teen to totally ignore this friend but to limit their conversations to a minute or so. It's acceptable to greet the friend and show an interest in him, but he must then move on.

4. *Be proactive.* Have your teen take the initiative to make plans with other friends before this friend can suggest plans.

5. *Be prepared to blame parents.* Let your teen know that he can respond to an invitation by honestly saying, "I'm really sorry, but my parents won't let me."

---

during the week I lead a different type of life. I'm kind and respectful toward others only if I feel like it. I don't pay much attention to whether my actions please God. It's not that I mind if others have a Christian commitment; that's their business. But I'd rather do what I want to do. Now, try pulling me up to your level."

While Gregory pulls up, his dad pulls down. You know who will win. The person with the lower position brings down the other. Before Gregory can pull his dad up, he'll be sprawled on the floor. It may not be "fair," but it's the way things are. It's much easier to pull someone down than to bring someone up.

"This is exactly what has happened between you and Haley," Gregory's dad explained. "You've tried to help her, but her choices and her parents' choices have made it so that she's pulling you down."

"But, Dad! I'm still the same me. I still care about God and good and right!"

"Yes, you do, but much of the light has gone out of your eyes. Anger is pushing away much that's good and right in you. You have separated yourself from most of your friends. You're even pulling away from your mom and me. And I can't remember the last time you enjoyed a game of softball."

"Softball players are stupid. And you're not being fair. If I want to make new friends, what business is it of yours?"

"There's nothing wrong with making new friends. But we're family, and what hurts you hurts your mom and me. It's true for adults and teenagers both: Some friends drag others down. I'm convinced that's what Haley's doing to you."

"She's not, Dad. I promise! I'll prove it to you!"

"I know you can. We're going to make some changes that will make it easier for you to show that you're not being overly influenced by Haley. First, you'll see her only one hour a week. Second, we need to work on your wardrobe."

"You said clothes are external only; they don't make a person good or bad!"

"That's true. But clothes do make a statement. And when you wear the chains and leather and all the dark clothing, you're saying to others: 'I'm angry, and I don't want to be involved with you.' "

"But that's not my real attitude!"

"Maybe not. But your appearance teaches people what to believe about you. It's not because they're mean; it's because those clothes characterize a person who is alienated from others. When you wear those clothes, people will have trouble seeing the friendly person you really are."

"So you admit that they're being judgmental!"

"This is not judgment; it's evaluation and discernment. The Bible says what's inside shows on the outside and what's outside tends to make its way toward the inside. It's a total package. You've got to choose to say with your demeanor and clothing what you believe on the inside [see Proverbs 15:13,30; 16:23]. And you need friends who will help you feel comfortable making those choices. Whoever you spend the most time with is the person you will imitate. If you hang with angry and sullen people, you'll end up acting angry and sullen."

"I'm not angry! Well, except at people who judge."

"Part of the reason you're reacting is because you know that you're judging the same people you claim are out to judge you. Being confronted with your own hypocrisy is scary. The other reason you're reacting is that you feel the same fear Haley feels. It's a desperate feeling of not knowing what to do with inner conflict and uncertainty. You can't escape being influenced by the people you hang out with. If they show anger, you'll start showing anger. That's why God was so picky about who the Israelites associated with in the Old Testament. It's the reason God encourages close friendships between practicing believers."

"I thought God wanted us to reach out."

"He does. But reaching out is not the same as developing close friendships. This is not snobbery; it's reality. Each of us becomes like the ones we spend time with. So we must carefully choose the friends we run with."

"Haley is a believer."

"But she is also making choices that don't honor God."

"Now you're judging!"

"Maybe so. In the same Bible passage, Jesus teaches not to judge but to refuse to throw your pearls to the pigs. There's a fine line between judgment and evaluating. I'll leave it up to God to decide. But I can honestly say that Haley is dragging you down."

"I don't agree, but let's leave Haley out of it. Why can't I dress like I want?"

"Because you're not dressing like you want. You're dressing like your group dresses."

"No I'm not! I make my own choices!"

"You just threw away the T-shirts you've been collecting for years. You bought those shirts with your own money at Christian rock concerts that you used to enjoy attending. Now, your black clothing and spiked jewelry is sending different messages. The last thing I want you to be is elitist about wearing only certain name brands. But you do need to choose more positive clothing. This weekend we'll go through your closet and choose what can stay and what must go. Monday you'll wear clothes that send positive signals."

"What will I say when people ask, 'Why the switch?'"

"You have several options. You can say your parents insisted that you change. You can say you decided to make a switch. Or you can lightly say 'a guy can choose what he wants to wear, and this is what I chose for today.'"

"I don't know, Dad."

"I understand that. But just trust me on this one. We'll work through it together."

I Don't Like My Teenager's Friends

Gregory's dad had chosen a difficult but necessary path. Gregory will buck and argue at every step. But as his parents remain consistent and as they affirm Gregory for each wise choice he makes, he'll eventually find his way to healthy friendships.

DEALING WITH A MORE REBELLIOUS TEENAGER

Even when they object to a parent's rules, most teenagers are secretly relieved that they are being steered away from destructive influences. Gregory felt trapped by Haley, and he knew her neediness was draining him, but he didn't see any other options. His parents' intervention came as a relief, although he didn't outwardly welcome their new rules.

Other teenagers aren't as self-aware. Faced with closer monitoring by their parents, they start sneaking out of the house and sneaking around behind their parents' backs. What should a parent do in those situations?

Even with a more rebellious teenager, parents must stay with the plan. It won't be easy, but their teen's present and future well-being depends on it. Parents have to repeat the reasons for the new rules, they have to continue to enforce the rules after repeated violations, and they have to affirm both large and small steps the teen makes toward healthy friendships. Why go to all this trouble? Because everything in your teen's life and well-being links to friendship.

If your teen is bold in his refusal to cut off damaging relationships and seek out more positive friendships, here are five actions that will help him pursue a healthier course:

1. *Explain the reasons behind your actions.* "Son, you need to know that all actions have consequences and nothing can truly be done in secret. I've seen you spend time with that individual even though we've forbidden you to do so. And even when

I don't see it, someone else does. The Bible says that what we do in secret will all come to light." (See Luke 8:17; Ecclesiastes 12:14.)

2. *Monitor your teen's actions.* Make it clear that you're going to follow through on this new plan. "I'd much rather you choose for yourself to build healthy relationships. But I will be watching to make certain you do. So let me catch you doing right."

3. *Direct your teen with proactive involvement.* Assure him that you will do whatever you can to help him succeed. "I'm committed to help guide you to the right path. If I have to, I'll spend the night in your room to keep you from sneaking out. We may have to go so far as to put a lock on your window while you sleep. I love you too much to let you ruin your life." (See Psalm 32:8-9.)

4. *Affirm his wise choices.* "Because you're choosing wisely, I'll let you use the car Friday night. We've gone a whole day without a challenge from my side or yours. I like the way you're taking charge." Be sure to acknowledge the steps he takes to develop positive friendships so he'll want to repeat them: "Your friendship with Jill shows great promise. Good choice on your part!"

5. *Repeat the steps above for as long as they are needed.* This difficulty won't be concluded in one series of encounters. You're teaching a life skill, not solving a short-term problem. So whenever it's needed, go back and repeat each step, especially in the areas of monitoring and directing.

Many parents do the explaining and the congratulating well, but they are unwilling to provide steady monitoring and direction. True, it takes time. True, you may have to miss an outing or repeated nights of sleep. True, your teen may deceive you into thinking that he's now following the rules only to return to his former patterns. So keep at it. If talking would solve all of our problems, parental lectures would be well loved! Teenagers need action. Careful monitoring during the teen years will pay off in self-monitoring for life.

Don't Rush Things

As Gregory's parents limited the time he could spend with Haley, Gregory understandably started to feel lonely. He expressed that loneliness as anger toward his parents. Fortunately, they recognized the anger for what it was and responded accordingly.

"Dad, I don't have any friends besides Haley. Why won't you let me go walking with her? We're not doing anything wrong. We don't even hold hands!"

"I know, Son. And I know you miss her companionship. There were some really good aspects to your friendship. But the bad overcame the good. Now we've got to fill that loneliness with other friends."

"But there's nobody else I want to be with."

"I understand that. But let's have one person over each weekend for a while. It doesn't have to be the same person, but little by little you'll bridge to different friends. Whoever you choose can come over Friday after school, Friday evening, or Saturday evening."

"But what would we do?"

"You could shoot baskets, play video games, make those milk shakes you like."

"Well, maybe Wes would come."

"Call him and see."

"What if he says, 'Last time I called, you wouldn't get together with me.' I wasn't exactly nice to him you know."

"I'd apologize. Or try to head that one off before it comes up. Just say, 'Wes, it's been too long since we got together. Would you mind starting over and doing something with me this weekend?'"

"He'd think I was some kind of wimp."

"He might. But he might not. Try it and see what happens."

Gregory was not born knowing how to rebuild friendships. Now that he's moving out of a destructive relationship, he needs his parents to show him how to rebuild his old friendships and cultivate new ones. Understanding that every teen needs adults other than his parents who care about him, they subtly invited parents of healthy teens to join the circle of adults who take an interest in Gregory. They didn't tell the story of Haley. They simply thanked them for their mentorship. In turn, they joined the group of caring adults who showed an interest in Gregory's old friends.

If you're working with your teen to rebuild healthy friendships, here's a *big caution:* Don't just throw a bunch of kids into a room and expect them to become buddies. Even kids with the best of characters will have trouble with this scenario. Some of my greatest nightmares as the mother of two teenagers have been parties with groups of good kids. Even though we provided games and get-to-know-you activities, the chemistry just wasn't there. So rather than begin with a large group, find out which friends click with your teen during "friend Fridays." It's easier for a kid to do things with one other teen than with a whole roomful of his peers. After you've given your teen a chance to build relationships one-on-one, build a party group from those connections. Keep adding to the group by regularly bringing new faces into future parties. Monitor things to see if the chemistry remains good with the addition of the newcomer. If things aren't gelling, have those who don't do as well in a group setting come over individually.

If your teen resists the idea of inviting a lot of kids over, his reluctance is understandable. The most common reason is the fear that the party will be boring. It's hard enough to worry about whether people like you, but if they also think coming to your house is a bore, that's a double whammy. Many teens won't risk it, but you can help.

First, show your teen's friends that you enjoy having them around.

No teen can resist another kid's parent who gives them attention and genuinely cares (they can tell!). Show this through listening to their stories. Learn the art of asking good questions like "Tell me about your week" and "What is your biggest dream in life?" Don't hang around too long. You're an adult, so act like one. But do give the kind of full-circle loving that reminds kids that someone who isn't their parent thinks they're pretty cool. Show them they're worth hearing and are fun to be around. Then tell them what you see: "I like the way you build others up during the game rather than try to win at all costs. That makes the game really fun." (See the chapter 1 sidebar "Top Talk Starters" for more questions.)

Second, show your teen how to party. Make lists of party foods, purchase party games (see the sidebar "Activities That Encourage Friendship" for ideas), and practice with small groups of two to four kids. Parties don't have to be rip-roaring to be good. Sharing a simple joke or hearing each other's stories is what teenagers long for. To avoid a sluggish event, work out a signal with your teen so you'll know when to help jump-start things. "Mom, will you bring more dip?" is a sample. You then casually stroll in and suggest a new game or give special attention to the party guests. Here are six easy ways to guide a teen's party without running the show:

- *Make sure each kid brings a snack.* This assures that the food is what the teens like. You'll need to have plenty of backup snacks, however.
- *Establish the no-put-down rule.* Make your home a safe haven, perhaps the only place on earth where kids don't have to fear getting flamed. If you hear a cutting remark, you can joke that you're weird about this, but you don't like anyone putting down anyone else in your home. They'll inwardly appreciate it and eventually will tease you back about it.
- *Be glad to take the blame.* Your teen can tell his friends, "You

know my mom. She's a party animal and always wants things happening at our house. So why don't you come over to make her happy?"

- *Stay close by.* Walk in and out of the party and say something nice to one or two guests each time. "I like your shirt." "That's a good strategy you're using in that game." Sometimes kids will ask you to stay, but don't stay more than a quarter of the time.

ACTIVITIES THAT ENCOURAGE FRIENDSHIP

You can't just throw a bunch of kids into a room and expect friendship to blossom. Most teenagers need activities that help them connect. Almost any shared activity will do the trick. Whether your group is two or two hundred, try these for starters:

- *Bake something.* Whether it's a store-bought mix or your family's trademark pizza recipe, give teenagers the ingredients and the recipe so they can get cooking.
- *Play a great game.* Our favorites include Beyond Balderdash, Cranium, Taboo, Pictionary, Guesstures, and Trivial Pursuit. All are designed for group interaction. Or play classic indoor games like spoons, charades, pencil charades, or card games.
- *Shoot baskets, practice soccer kicks, or play catch.* Or set up the volleyball net, badminton net, or croquet set.
- *Serve at a clothes closet, shelter, or other service spot.* Invite a friend along while you and your teen serve.
- *Study together.* If your teen has to work, he might as well have company. Pick genuine studiers, and check on them frequently.
- *Leave off the television and VCR.* Watching movies together teaches teens about the movie rather than about each other. Save the movies for when the slumber party gets late and you want to coax the group to sleep.

- *Stay awake until the party ends.* When kids know you're nearby, any temptation toward orneriness will fade. This is particularly important when your teen has a date in the house.
- *Stay within earshot.* You not only get to enjoy the giggles of pure togetherness, but you can walk in without your teenager's signal if things get stale.

PITCH IN WITH LOVE

The best friendships are those with kids from healthy families since the parents from those families love your teenager just as you love theirs. This doesn't mean you build an exclusive group of happy kids. It means you encourage your teen to spend the greatest amount of time with other healthy friends, and you show your son or daughter why this is important. Here's how it worked out between Gregory and his dad.

"I'm sad that you and Doug never got back together, but I'm glad you've started spending more time with Wes."

"Me, too. His mom is so funny. She says something cool to me every time I go over there."

"Yeah? Like what?"

"Like, 'Gregory, you are the best looking man in your grade (next to my Wesley, of course). It's no wonder you two have trouble getting girls' attention sometimes. Your good looks overwhelm them!'"

"That's true!"

"Oh, Dad. You know I have trouble getting dates because I'm so shy."

"Not always. In fact, I can name five girls that you've mentioned talking with just this week. Any guy who can talk to five different girls is anything but shy!"

"Thanks. But I'm not so sure."

"That's okay. But I gotta tell you why I like your spending time with Wes and his sister. They and their mom bring out the best in you."

"What do you mean?"

"Well, as you just said, Wes's mom is always teasing you in ways that remind you how valuable you are. And Wendy and you can talk without feeling weird. Wes can challenge and encourage you at the same time."

"But isn't it selfish to want friends who make me feel good?"

"Only if you're not doing the same for them. Mutuality is critical to strong friendships. It's more than feeling good—it's being competent and prepared for life. It's also having the confidence to do the right thing. The Bible calls it 'iron sharpening iron' [see Proverbs 27:17]. You have to be strong to sharpen someone."

"But I used to sharpen Haley. I still don't see why you won't let me see her more."

"Because that friendship wasn't mutual. To sharpen each other you *both* have to be strong. Haley just doesn't have the family support to be a good friend to you right now."

"But her parents go to church!"

"They've made the right choice there but the wrong choices in how they raise—or neglect to raise—Haley. As a consequence, her weakness overpowers her."

"Well, who helps the weak people then?"

"You and Wes and I and others."

"So can I see Haley more?"

"No. She needs parenting, and you can't give that to her. You can give her encouragement from the side, and I can give some of that too. Several people can take an interest in her and show her love. It has to be a team effort. With too much individual contact, she'll bring that one person down. You alone can't bring her up. It's just the way things work—she looks to you for what her parents are supposed to give. And you can't give that."

"But it's not fair to Haley."

"I agree. This is one of those sad realities of life that are beyond our control."

To his dad's amazement, Gregory didn't always buck when his dad limited the time he could spend with Haley. It became clear that he was enjoying his time with old friends like Wes and Wendy. Without his parents' intervention, he would have missed out on those affirming friendships.

When your teen bucks, remember that rage and sullenness have

BOOKS THAT DEMONSTRATE HEALTHY FRIENDSHIPS

As you show your teens how to build good friendships, let quality novels help. Of course you won't say, "Here's a book that will show you the right way to live." Instead, you'll give the first book in a series and say, "I've heard these books are good. Let me know what you think."

Fast Forward to Normal, by Jane Vogel and others in the Brio Girls series (published by Focus on the Family).

Tornado Alley, by Yvonne Lehman and others in the White Dove Romance series (Bethany House).

Summer Promise, by Robin Jones Gunn and others in the Christy Miller series or Sierra Jenson series (Focus on the Family).

Secrets, by Robin Jones Gunn and others in the Glenbrooke series (especially for older teens, by Multnomah).

Abandoned on the Wild Frontier, by Dave and Neta Jackson and others in the Trailblazer series (Bethany House).

Too Many Secrets, by Patricia Rushford and others in the Jennie their roots in fear and uncertainty. As you give your teenager boundaries and security, you push away those dark experiences. Your teens become free to invest confidently in healthy friendships, and they begin to make use of the gifts God has given them.

Left to their own decisions, many teenagers would never learn the richness and blessing of healthy friendships. This is the essence of good parenting—showing your kids how and why to build solid friendships. You open your home, you monitor the relationships, you affirm your teen's wise choices, and you guide him away from bad choices. It's a process that's agonizingly tough and requires wearying consistency, but it brings rich results.

McGrady mystery series (especially for younger teens, by Bethany House).

Risky Assignment, by Judy Baer and others in the Live from Brentwood High series (Bethany House).

The Shunning, by Beverly Lewis and others in the Heritage of Lancaster County series (especially for older teens, by Bethany House).

The Misfit, The Trick, The Rescue, or *The Rebel*, by Nancy Rue and others in the Christian Heritage series (Bethany House).

Choice Summer, by Shirley Brinkerhoff and others in the Nikki Sheridan series (Bethany House).

Don't Count on Homecoming Queen, by Nancy Rue and others in the Raise the Flag series (WaterBrook).

Daughters of Twin Oaks, by Lauraine Snelling and others in the Secret Refuge or Red River of the North series (especially for older teens, by Bethany House).

Tripping Over Skyscrapers, by Wendy Nentwig and others in the Unmistakably Cooper Ellis series (Bethany House).

ACTION STEPS

You can guide your teens to choose good friends. This is not control; it's showing them how to discern character in others. Remember, no one is born knowing how to recognize the good and bad in people. You'll have to show your teen how and why.

What Scripture says: "Bad company corrupts good character" (1 Corinthians 15:33). Conversely good friends give each other the power to choose well and refuse evil. "Though one may be overpowered, two can defend themselves" (Ecclesiastes 4:12).

Explain to your teen: "There's only so much of you to go around. Choose friends who will cherish you and bring out the best in you. Only then can you fulfill God's purposes for your life. Then do the same for your friends."

[3]

MY TEENAGER THINKS ONLY OF HIMSELF

IT'S A MISTAKE TO LET THE "LITTLE THINGS" SLIDE

When Eliza's first grader, Kym, poured sugar packets all over the table at a restaurant, she wasn't concerned that the waitress would have to clean up the mess. After all, Kym was just a little girl. She meant no harm. She even shaped the sugar into little scenes. Maybe it was an expression of her artistic bent.

"If that's the worst thing she ever does," Eliza said, "I have nothing to worry about."

Now a teenager, Kym leaves her dirty clothes scattered all over her room and her sculpting tools all over the garage. She doesn't mean any harm; she just has an extremely busy schedule and little time to pick up after herself. So Eliza goes through the house cleaning up after her daughter. Even with her mom's help, though, several of Kym's sculpting tools have gotten lost. Others have rusted. And some of her tossed-aside clothes have been ruined.

Kym's carelessness is starting to cause problems. Her mom can see that it's not just the expression of an artistic kid, but a lack of care and an avoidance of responsibility. What should Eliza do to help her daughter be more aware of how her actions affect others? She can start by showing Kym how to grow in considering others as well as herself.

45

Without responsibility, Kym will find it hard to live with herself, and others will find it hard to be around her.

Eliza understands with her head that individual ingredients make the whole. As a graphic designer, she recognizes that the big picture comes from millions of tiny pixels. But in parenting, she overlooks the same truth. Rather than recognize that a teenager's small habits combine to produce a complete person—either good or bad—she prefers to pick her parenting battles. She makes excuses for Kym's careless habits, saying they aren't worth worrying about.

When designing an illustration on the computer, would Eliza claim that she could pick any colors she wants when creating an ocean scene? Would it make the result stronger if she hopes and prays for a good outcome? Of course not. She must keep the big picture in mind and select colors in proper proportions to create the desired result. Her intentions don't matter; her actual choices do. It works the same in parenting. Each encounter with Kym is a chance for Eliza to add pixels of guidance, affirmation, and explanation. Wishing and hoping—even praying—won't do it. Only action will work in this situation.

Parents must build into their teenagers' lives the specific virtues that produce godly character: love, joy, peace, patience, kindness, goodness, faithfulness, gentleness, and self-control (see Galatians 5:22-23). These are the virtues that power a successful life. Little actions become habits, habits become character traits, and character traits become lifestyles. Each action and reaction matters. That's why we must insist that our teens express the essential virtues in their character. Otherwise they will fail at life.

Is it possible to build virtue into a teenager's character? Absolutely. That's the essence of parenting. We parents must deliberately guide, teach, and practice. As Eliza observes Kym's careless and self-centered habits, she must recognize that no issues are too small and no behaviors

A PICTURE OF GOOD CHARACTER

To develop your child's character, you must recognize how the small pieces combine to form the big picture. Here are five ways to do just that.

1. Ponder what the world would be like if everyone behaved like your teenager at this moment. If the world would be better, praise that behavior. If the world would be worse, get your teen to stop the behavior.

2. See this process as nurture rather than control, because guiding and directing really are nurturing.

3. Handle each behavior in ways that paint God's picture rather than muddy it.

4. Recognize that what your teen practices today will show up in his or her character as an adult. Don't freak over every behavior, but do handle it. For example, when your teen calls his brother stupid, don't launch into lectures about good words. Just firmly say, "In this family we do not put down one another. Say three kind things to your brother. Then to keep you from saying ugly things to him again, know that you'll lose an hour of computer time for every unkind word you speak." Then take away computer time when it happens again (because it will).

5. Use the fruit of the Holy Spirit as your frame of reference (see Galatians 5:22-23). For instance, to be considerate requires that you *patiently* take time to hear that the other person needs to be in the bathroom so she can catch the bus; that you *kindly* cooperate to share the bathroom mirror; that you show goodness by refusing to argue over bathroom time—instead you set a timer.

too insignificant to address. No matter how lax she has been in the past, Eliza must start today to deliberately shape her daughter into the godly woman God designed her to become.

Keep the Big Picture in View

Your teenager, like Kym, is an unfinished work of art. God has entrusted parents with the skills and the colors to paint our teenagers' character. These colors include the fruit of the Holy Spirit, the Ten Commandments, and more. The ultimate goal is a picture of Christ-likeness, not boys who will be boys or girls who just wanna have fun. When it comes to character, there are no "little things."

Kym's big picture has been muddied by self-centeredness. She's not deliberately being careless; she just doesn't pay attention to how her actions affect others. It's a brand of selfishness that gradually eats away at all that is good in life. It needs to be replaced by intentional goodness. Kym needs huge strokes of a biblical command to "look not only to your own interests, but also to the interests of others" (Philippians 2:4).

This same command is just as important for Kym's mom. Continuing to pick up after Kym will teach Kym to look out only for herself. Eliza must change her parenting patterns so Kym can change her own habits. The first parenting pattern for Eliza to change is how she reacts to Kym's carelessness.

When Eliza becomes frustrated, she sometimes resorts to lecturing. Kym just tunes her out because she knows her mom's words mean nothing. Eliza has tried leaving Kym's clothing and tools wherever her daughter drops them. Kym just steps over the stuff, because she knows her mom will pick them up eventually. Eliza has also tried restricting Kym's privileges, but Kym knows the restrictions won't last.

The critical element missing in all this is the parental art of demonstration. Eliza must not just tell Kym what to do, she must show her. It takes only a second more for Kym to carry her clothes to the hamper. So Eliza must shift her lecture from "Why do you keep leaving your stuff on the floor?" to "Here's what will happen if you drop your stuff on the floor."

She will explain, "We live in the same space, and that means we must look out not only for our own needs but also the needs of others. Quite simply, that means you pick up your stuff and I'll pick up mine. It just takes a second more to walk it to the hamper."

Eliza's explanation will lead to positive results only if she consistently follows her words with actions that show Kym how it works. She must demonstrate the consequences by leaving Kym's stuff wherever she drops it, but this time leaving it there long enough to make a difference in her daughter's habits. She must choose natural consequences rather than punishments that are so random that Kym knows the chances of getting in trouble are slim.

Here's an example of demonstrating the natural consequences of a self-centered habit:

"Kym, beginning today I need you to put your laundry in the hamper and put away any tools you use in the garage."

"I'd be glad to, Mom, but not this week. I have too much going on."

"Everybody is busy. So you must learn patterns that get the chores done along with the scheduled stuff."

"You never made me do this before. When did you become such a neat freak?"

"I've been wrong to pick up after you. From now on, you'll get your clothes to the laundry basket, or they won't get washed. I'll wash any clothes that are in the basket by 6 A.M. on laundry days. You'll replace with your own money any clothes that mildew or any tools that get rusty or are lost."

"But, Mom, you have more time than I do. Why can't you take care of my laundry and tools if I forget once or twice?"

"Because each person's cleaning up her own messes is part of living together. The Bible calls it goodness—doing good things for the others you live with." (Eliza doesn't waste time arguing who has more time, because that's not the point.)

"Mom, I agree with all that. *You* can be good to *me* by picking up my stuff. My room is on your way to the laundry room."

"Exactly. And you can express your goodness by taking your clothes a few steps farther. One-sided goodness allows the other person to be selfish. I won't allow you to make a habit of selfishness."

"I told you, I don't have time!"

"So what would you like to drop from your schedule?"

"Taking the laundry to the hamper."

"Sorry. It only takes a couple seconds to walk to the hamper."

Kym ends the conversation with an apathetic "whatever" and carries the clothes that are lying on her floor to the hamper. Eliza sighs in relief.

But by the end of the week, Kym's floor is again covered. The perspiration in her soccer uniform makes her bedroom smell like a locker room. She complains on Friday afternoon, "Mom! My blue jersey isn't in my closet. I have to wear it tonight. Where is it?"

"Check your floor."

"Mom, you *know* I have to have a clean jersey or the coach will penalize me."

"I know that. And you know that if the clothes are not in the hamper they don't get washed."

"Is there time to wash it before the game?"

"You can try."

"Mom, why are you doing this to me?"

"I'm not doing it to you; you're doing it to yourself. You chose to leave your clothes on the floor."

"But why are you choosing not to help me?"

"So you'll express goodness. It takes thinking ahead and intentional action. Goodness is a fruit of the Holy Spirit, and it's up to me as your mom to help you practice patterns of goodness."

"I'm glad to get some practice, but not at the expense of a clean jersey!"

"That's my opinion too. Expensive jerseys shouldn't be left on the floor."

"You are so unfair!"

LEARNING RULES FROM MEAN MOTHER SCHOOL

When parents enforce rules, teens often accuse them of being mean. Good parents earn A's in "mean" when *mean* signifies following through, explaining the rules rather than being a boss, and remembering to tell your teenagers the *why* with the *what:*

- "I make you treat your sister nicely so you will learn patterns of peace and togetherness."
- "I make you do chores because chores are part of life. If you don't do your share, you're a mooch; if you do them all, you're a slave. So we each do our share."
- "I make you check in so you'll know that someone cares enough to know where you are."
- "I insist on meeting your friends so I can express pride in your good choices."
- "I make you take turns so people will want to be around you."
- "I show you how to get everything done because everyone has the same twenty-four hours in a day."
- "I praise your self-control because through that you can ward off temptation and move past obstacles to choose what you really want."

Sound familiar? When the accusations begin, don't yell, don't argue, and don't say "I told you so." Just calmly allow the natural consequences to unfold.

Express Faith, Not Your Immediate Feelings

Eliza feels horrible. Kym's coach really will penalize her for not having a clean jersey. Maybe she has been a bit too hard on her daughter. It's just a jersey, after all. And Kym is only fifteen. Everyone knows that teenagers are naturally messy.

Time out!

If Eliza gives in now, Kym will continue to ruin clothing and to lose tools, continue to expect others to wait on her, continue to assume that she's too busy to do the dull stuff of life. And she will hurt others all along the way. Initially, it will be easier for Eliza to make excuses for her daughter, but it will be easier in the long run if she does the harder thing *now*. She needs to follow through on enforcing the laundry rule.

Rather than act on her feelings that Kym's occasional carelessness should be overlooked, Eliza must put her faith into motion. Excuses like "This is not a big deal" or "I have to pick my battles" sound like logical alternatives to conflict. But in reality, *everything* is a big deal when it comes to molding a God-honoring person. Parenting is faith in action. Every action either brings your teenager closer to a picture of Christlikeness or moves your teen farther away from it. We don't have to make mountains out of molehills, but we do have to address the molehills.

God is the power source for all of this to happen, but parents are the catalysts who turn on the power. The good news is that a few battles at the start will go far in smoothing things out during most of the teenage years. The bad news is that ignoring even the tiniest troublesome behavior allows it to grow into huge storms that will pelt you and your teenager with indescribable horrors: hurtful words, self-centeredness, rebellion, lack of self-discipline, griping, loneliness, and alienation. If you refuse to teach your children Christlike character, their pain and the pain of their children will persist for generations (see Numbers 14:18). But if you are consistent in teaching your kids biblical virtues, the benefits continue even more powerfully in subsequent generations (see Psalm 78:4-8).

WHAT A PARENT SAYS AND WHAT REALLY COMES ACROSS

Too often we parents say things that sound wise or logical, but in effect we simply give an excuse for neglecting our parental responsibility. Consider the following:

"Boys will be boys" really means "The rules are different for boys. Girls have to behave; boys don't."

"I have to choose my battles" really means "Only certain behaviors are important to God. Everyday life doesn't matter to him."

"She made her bed; now she can lie in it" really means "I'm avoiding the hard work of turning my teen back to the right path."

"I quit trying to control him long ago" really means "I let him be more powerful than I am."

"She said she doesn't want my advice, so I let her take care of things" really means "I don't want to put up with the discomfort of giving and following through with difficult advice."

"All I can do is pray" really means "I don't want to be bothered with parenting. I'd rather not stay home and keep my teen and her boyfriend from temptation."

Parenting takes perseverance and courage. Eliza must stand firm. She doesn't want Kym to be an irresponsible, self-centered teenager, but a young woman who imitates Jesus Christ. As Jesus worked in the carpenter shop, he persisted through splinters and scorching summer afternoons to learn the trade his stepfather was teaching him. In so doing, he "grew in wisdom and stature, and in favor with God and men" (Luke 2:52). If God himself could live on earth doing the daily stuff of life well, Kym can too.

Eliza takes a deep breath, prays for strength, and then lets Kym decide whether to wear the sweaty, wrinkled jersey or go to the soccer game wearing a washed-but-wet shirt. She will let Kym plan what to say to the coach, encouraging honesty: "Tell him what actually happened—that you didn't get it washed." She will let Kym experience the consequences of her actions: the penalty from the coach, the embarrassment of showing up in a smelly or wet jersey, the panic of not knowing what to do.

After Kym leaves for the game, her mom will agonize in private. But no matter how bad she feels, she must resist the temptation to call the coach and explain that it was really her fault. It wasn't. She'll remind herself that only through such experiences can Kym's portrait change from one of irresponsibility to responsibility, from selfishness to goodness. She'll recognize that Kym just might put her jersey in the hamper next time so she can go to soccer wearing a clean jersey and enjoy the triumph of taking care of her things.

Even harder, the training-up-her-child-in-the-way-she-should-go process is not over. Developing Christlike character doesn't happen in one encounter any more than a computer image is created with just one keystroke. Kym whines on her way out the door the following Friday morning, "Won't you *please* take care of my jersey just this once? I have two before-school meetings!" Eliza again prays for strength and then explains, "I'm going to treat you like a responsible person. All of us are busy and all of us have to find time to do the mundane things. You can wash your jersey after school if you need to."

"But, Mom!"

"I'm helping you develop habits of goodness and self-control. As you practice those, you can enjoy the good results."

"Mom, you're impossible!" Kym says as she treks back to pick up the jersey and take it to the laundry hamper.

"I got high grades in Impossible at mother school."

Notice there is no yelling and no arguing. No guilt producing or criticizing. Those are unnecessary and counterproductive. Just calmly show and calmly tell. That's enough to get the message across.

WHY BOTHER WITH THE SMALL STUFF?

By making an issue out of the "small things," Eliza is helping her daughter avoid creating pain for others. In the past, Eliza has been the first recipient of that pain—being treated like a slave rather than a mom. No matter how much she invests in her daughter's clothes and sculpture tools, Kym will regard them as expendable if Eliza doesn't help her change her patterns. Eventually Kym will treat her college roommate and finally her husband in the same thoughtless way. She'll make messes wherever she goes. Some teenagers take self-centeredness to an extreme, committing criminal acts because they care so little about others.

Why do little things like laundry mean so much? Shouldn't we worry more about whether Kym gets to work on time or how she treats her siblings? We should worry about *all* of it, since each behavior connects to the others. Picking up laundry makes Kym more sensitive to the needs of her sister who shares her room. Treating siblings well helps Kym want to carry her share of the load at her part-time job. Taking her share of the workload will result in whacking thirty minutes off the usual closing time. Saving half an hour on closing means she can come home and tell her sibling, who's now become a friend, about the cute customer she got to wait on. And life becomes good.

Remember the big picture—keystrokes that create a portrait of Christlike character. Our teens must accept Jesus Christ as their Savior and Lord before they will fully grasp how and why to live for him. But our teaching along the way works hand-in-hand with God to draw them to him and then to show them how to honor him.

Getting the small things right pays off when a teenager starts getting the big things right. Eliza noticed that as Kym started taking more care with her laundry and her sculpting tools, she was also becoming more considerate of others.

"Kym, you show such love and patience to your brother when you listen like that. You make him feel like he's the only person in the world."

"It's no big deal."

"No, really it is. You held back your story to hear his. Then you honored him by telling your story. The way you treat the people you live with is a great testimony to whether you honor or dishonor God."

"Cool. Thanks, Mom."

Raising Kym is more than telling her what she does wrong, more than correcting her shortcomings. It includes acknowledging what she does well. Develop the habit of affirming some way that your teenager demonstrates a fruit of the Holy Spirit every day (see sidebar "Your Christlike Character Shows"). As you point out the ways your teen is successful in living for Jesus, she will be even more motivated to repeat that success.

In helping to guide Kym, Eliza has been great at affirmation, but she hasn't always affirmed the right things. When Kym was little, her mom saw art in the sugar sculptures she made at restaurants rather than see the spilled sugar as a way to saddle a hard-working waitress with one more unnecessary chore. So Eliza must begin finding truly good actions and attitudes that specifically relate to the fruit of the Holy Spirit. She must not call bad behavior good just to sound nice. Eliza must learn the pattern of genuine praise. The more she praises Kym for

---

YOUR CHRISTLIKE CHARACTER SHOWS

Your teens are not born knowing how to paint a Christlike character in their own lives. They need you to show them how to do it and to make it known when they succeed. To prompt yourself to regularly mention a way they live out the fruit of the Spirit, keep a tally. Here are sample ways to say it:

- "Kym, your friendliness to new students is a great demonstration of God's *love*."
- "Jason, you sow *joy* in the Bible study when you affirm each person's comment."
- "Kym, talking directly about that problem helped you keep *peace* rather than create tension."
- "Jason, you chose *patience* when you stopped before smashing the wall in frustration. Good choice!"
- "Kym, you slowed down and waited for your sister like you would have wanted her to do for you. That's *kindness*."
- "Jason, refusing to hog the bathroom shows *goodness* to your sister. I won't let her hog it either."
- "Kym, refusing to put down a person expresses *faith* that each person, whom God created, matters."
- "Jason, it's hard for a guy to be *gentle,* but you do it with such strength."
- "Kym, you showed godly *self-control* when that player deliberately kicked you. Way to be like Jesus!"

---

the things that please God, the more Kym will want to please her and to please God, too.

Keep It Balanced

Just like complementary colors plus darks and lights make a picture look complete, you must include three shades in your parenting picture: affirmation, correction, and explanation.

Affirmation is a great starting point, but it must be balanced with correction. Affirming without correcting makes you a lazy parent. Affirmation alone means you are choosing not to show the gumption that will take your teen to the next level; you're only noticing what your teen has already learned. When you do that, you leave it up to others to raise your teenager.

Correction also needs to be exercised in balance to keep it from becoming oppression. Correction without explanation makes your parenting a matter of control. When you issue rules without explaining them, your kids don't learn to think for themselves. When they leave home they'll experiment with everything you told them to avoid because they saw only oppression in your rules. But if you show them how certain behaviors affect other people and impact the world for Christ, they'll want to continue those patterns on their own.

Explanation, the third essential, needs to be given in balance with both affirmation and correction. In a vacuum, explanation makes you nothing more than a talking head—all noise, no action. A teenager can see right through anyone who says he believes something but then doesn't back it up with actions. True Christian parenting needs the why (explanation), the how (correction), and the congratulations (affirmation). When you parent in balance, your teens will have the understanding to know how to choose for themselves to paint their lives in the image of Jesus Christ.

ACTION STEPS

A teen's bad behavior isn't something you excuse to keep from making your son or daughter sad. Wrong actions and attitudes are what make your teenagers sad. So treat every action and reaction like it matters. Refuse to ignore wrong behavior. Instead teach your teens how and why to embrace right behavior.

What Scripture says:

> I will instruct you and teach you in the way you should go;
>> I will counsel you and watch over you.
> Do not be like the horse or the mule,
>> which have no understanding
> but must be controlled by bit and bridle. (Psalm 32:8-9)

Explain to your teen: "Nobody is born knowing how. So I'll show my love the same way God loves, by teaching why certain actions, attitudes, and words honor or dishonor him. Then you can know how to choose to honor God on your own."

4

MY TEENAGER WON'T DO
HER HOMEWORK

REPLACE IRRESPONSIBILITY
WITH SELF-DISCIPLINE

"Jessie, do your homework. You have that party tonight and then church in the morning. So go ahead and get it done."

"I will, Dad. Just let me finish this video game."

"The *minute* the game is over, I want you starting."

"No problem, Dad."

Just then the phone rings.

"I'll get it!" Jessie calls. An hour later she is still on the phone, which prompts another reminder from her dad.

"Jessie, you need to do your homework!" Jessie puts her hand over the phone and, incredulous that her dad doesn't understand, says, "But this is *important*. Jen has a problem, and she needs to talk it through!"

Her dad feels bad for interrupting his daughter when she's helping a hurting friend, so he backs sheepishly out of Jessie's room.

Another half-hour passes and the phone is still in use. Jessie's dad needs to get on the Internet, but he paces the floor instead. He knocks on Jessie's door, only to have her throw a slipper. Again she puts her hand over the phone and whispers with urgency, "Dad, *please*. Jen needs to talk!"

It's true that Jessie's friend needs to talk, but Jessie also needs to do her homework. She'll be leaving for a party in only ninety minutes. And her dad needs to e-mail some work to a colleague. So he whispers, holding up five fingers, "Five more minutes."

Jessie rolls her eyes and scribbles on a notepad: "You can't put a time limit on a personal crisis!" She pitches the notepad at her dad.

It's time for another viewpoint, so Jessie's dad asks his wife what to do. "Your guess is as good as mine," she tells him. "I can never get her off the phone either."

After the promised five minutes and more have passed, Jessie's dad knocks on the door, grabs the phone, and says to Jessie's friend: "Sorry, Jen, but Jessie has to do her homework because she's leaving in a little while and has church activities all day tomorrow. She'll see you at school on Monday."

"Dad!" Jessie screams. "How could you embarrass me like that?"

"I don't want to embarrass you, but you have to do your homework, and I have to get online. I realize Jen is in some sort of crisis, but we have to clear the phone line. Let me know when your homework is done, and if there's still time before the party, you can call her back."

Dad goes to his office and logs on. As he sends files to his coworker and checks his e-mail, he loses track of time. An hour later he goes back to his daughter's room expecting to see her buried in the books. She has a big research project due on Monday, but her books are closed and she's watching television.

"Jessie, why aren't you studying?"

"You made me mad, and you know I can't concentrate when I'm mad. So I turned on the game to calm down."

"Well, you've had plenty of time to get calm. Turn it off and hit the books."

"But, Dad, there are only five minutes left in the game!"

"Five minutes can become thirty with all the time-outs. Turn it off now."

"I will, Dad. I will. Just five real minutes."

Dad leaves. The next sound he hears is the shower running. Standing outside the bathroom door, he asks: "Jessie, is your homework done?"

"No, Dad. But I have to get ready. I'll do my homework after the party."

"No. You'll do it *before* the party. It won't hurt you to arrive a little late."

"Dad! You told me to bring Serena to help her feel part of the group. She finally agreed to come. If I don't show, all my efforts will be down the drain!"

Jessie's dad backs down again, not wanting to discourage his daughter's compassion. Serena is a new girl who needs to plug into a good group. When Jessie gets home from the party later that night, she is so wound up that it takes her forty-five minutes to get settled. By then, it's late. So she goes to bed without getting to her research project, saying she needs some sleep before church in the morning. The next day is busy with church, then Jessie goes to a movie with Serena, convinced that she can win her friend to Christ if they just spend some time together.

Jessie's dad is torn between two good things: Schoolwork is important, but so are his daughter's efforts at reaching out to an unchurched friend.

"Jessie, you've done a good thing by spending the afternoon with Serena. Now you're gonna have to skip youth group and finish that homework."

"But, Dad, I can't miss youth group! You know I need to keep in touch with my Christian friends."

Her dad reneges, and Jessie leaves the house again. She returns by nine, and at midnight she still isn't finished with the research project. Her dad concludes that he can't *make* Jessie do her homework, so he goes to bed. Jessie finally falls asleep at her desk, waking up early the next morning with a headache and in a terrible mood. She realizes that she'll have to turn the project in late. Her teacher enforces a strict rule on late assignments—a loss of one letter grade. Jessie's grades are already suffering, and this won't help.

DELIBERATELY IMPART THE NEEDED SKILLS

Jessie's dad can't figure out how to make his daughter buckle down and do her homework. He's tried everything he can think of, and nothing seems to work. If you have a Jessie in your family, don't despair. There are solutions to this dilemma. Begin by rejecting the myth that homework is one of those things you can't make your teen do. You've heard that you can lead a horse to water, but you can't make him drink. That's not the whole story. If you feed the horse enough salt, he'll want to drink that water! The same principle applies to homework: Feed your teen some salt.

The best salt to use varies from one teenager to the next, but it usually touches on some form of freedom. Teenagers treasure the freedom to go out with friends, to read, to talk on the phone, to use e-mail or instant messaging, to play their favorite music. That makes freedom a perfect motivator for most teens.

Once your teen finishes her homework, she can have freedom. For Jessie, that means playing a video game, talking to Jen on the phone, or watching sports on television. Her parents can use these freedoms to encourage more diligence in completing homework assignments. Rather than start her homework "as soon as I get to the next level on this video game," "as soon as the game is over," or "as soon as I solve Jen's crisis," her parents must insist that Jessie not even begin those activities until her homework is completed. The new rule is "After your homework is done, you'll be free to call Jen." Jessie will know that she'd better get her homework done if she hopes to ever use the phone again or watch the end of a televised game.

Whether your teen is an occasional dawdler or a chronic homework avoider, this advice might sound too simplistic. You might be thinking, *My teen would* never *go for this!*

Welcome to the club. In twenty-eight years of youth ministry, I've never met a teenager who applauds a parent for enforcing uncomfortable rules. And I've not yet met a teen who will do her homework without someone pressing the issue. Teens make it known how unhappy they are when parents present restrictions, but they eventually grow to respect these parents and to choose the responsible behavior that complies with the rules.

The answer? Give the guidance teens need. To make this work, you'll have to make the new rules clear and consistently enforce them. Motivate yourself by recognizing that your teen's homework is important not only for the present, but it is also a great practice ground for developing the skills she'll need to succeed in life. In completing her homework, she'll learn time management, focusing skills, commitment to getting the hard stuff done no matter how distasteful, and good work habits. These are the very skills that will enable her to build a marriage, keep a job, raise her children, and manage a home. So do your child a favor and show her how to get her homework done.

No one is born with excellent organizational skills; we all have to learn how to get our work done efficiently. Your teenager might well have more homework assignments than you had at her age, and she might feel overwhelmed by the workload. So help your teen break the task down into smaller pieces. Homework training includes listing the assignments, breaking down the bigger projects into manageable segments, setting deadlines for completing each stage of the project, and

It's More Than Homework

If I make my teenager do his homework before having fun, he'll learn that work comes before pleasure.

But if I don't make my teenager do his homework, he'll learn that he only has to do what he feels like doing.

If I make my teen do her homework first no matter how much is going on, she'll learn that she can fit all good things into the time she has available.

But if I don't make my teen do her homework, she'll use "I didn't have time" as an excuse for not doing church, family time, work, and the other good things of life.

If I make my teenager do his homework, he'll learn that good comes through obeying authority figures (and the primary authority is God).

But if I don't make my teenager do his homework, he'll learn he can ignore authority figures except when it's convenient.

If I make my teenager do her homework first, she'll discover the security of routine.

But if I don't make my teenager do her homework, she'll flit from one distraction to another and never accomplish anything.

If I make my teenager do his homework, he'll learn that doing the hard thing now results in good things later on, such as higher grades or a scholarship to a better college.

But if I don't make my teenager do his homework, he'll lack self-discipline and be prone to such feel-good-constantly measures as drug use, overeating, and more.

monitoring to make certain each step gets done on time. For big projects, like a major research paper, it might help to assign the work to certain times of the weekend. Here's how Jessie's parents helped her develop better time-management skills.

"Jessie, what homework do you have this weekend?"

"Oh, not much really."

"Walk me through a list of what has to be done before Monday."

"I need to finish a history report, study for a math test, and review a couple of chapters for English."

"How long is the report?"

"What is this, the Inquisition?"

"No, it's actually a plan to keep me from nagging you about homework. You'll like this approach much better, believe me. We're going to formulate a plan."

"Oh, I won't need all that. I've got it covered. Don't worry."

"I know you think it's covered. But last weekend, you were up past midnight with your research paper and still turned it in late. We're not going to repeat that scenario."

"But last weekend was really busy. This weekend won't be so bad."

"Maybe not, or it may be even busier. In either case we'll work together to be certain your homework is done before Sunday. So before you make any phone calls on Saturday, I want you to have reviewed those two chapters for English and also to have studied for the math test. Finish those, and you can call Jen. Then, before you go out on Saturday night, I want to see your history report, complete and printed out. I'll quiz you on the chapters and the material for the test to make certain you've studied. I'll read your report to make sure the content is strong and that you didn't miss any typos."

"Dad, I know how to do homework! I don't need a baby-sitter."

"I understand that. But life can crowd out the time you reserve for homework, so we're making certain you get it done before Sunday. My checking will keep you from the temptation to tell me it's done when it's not."

"I have Sunday afternoon. Why can't I do it then?"

"Because if someone invites you out or you have an extra meeting at church, I don't want you staying up late on Sunday night. And sometimes homework takes longer than we think it will. Pacing your work to finish by Saturday night gives you a bit of a cushion. Besides all that, not doing homework on Sunday will be a good way to 'honor the Sabbath.'"

"Well, didn't we get holy all of a sudden!"

"Jessie, be respectful. I know this is a big change. It's different for me, too, because I'll have to remind myself not to nag you. But I'm giving you the rest of the afternoon and evening today and all day tomorrow to get a few hours of homework done. That's more than enough time."

"Easy for you to say."

"Yes it is. But it's the same way I plan out my work projects. Now when do you have to have your homework done?"

"Before I go out on Saturday."

"And two of the assignments have to be done before you talk on the phone. If you don't finish, you can stay in Saturday until it's finished."

"Do I have to do it right now?" Jessie asks, not wanting to spoil her Friday afternoon.

"Whatever it takes to get it done by Saturday night."

"I'm waiting until tomorrow."

"That's up to you, as long as you get everything done by tomorrow night."

Remember to tell your teenager that she's not deliberately doing anything wrong with her time; she just hasn't figured out how to get done what needs to be done. If she continues practicing poor time-management habits, she'll give her second best to God and she won't be making the most of the life he's given to her. There is time for work and time for fun, and its much easier to reward completed work with the fun than to pull away from the fun to do the work.

Keep feeding salt and then showing your teenager how to drink.

REFINE THOSE SKILLS

As you teach your teenager the important life skill of time management, make sure you don't start thinking of it as showing your son or daughter who's in control. Getting homework and other chores done is not a control thing, it's a process in developing needed life skills. It's also the only way a teenager can learn to get both the fun things and the not-so-fun things done.

STEPS THAT TEACH SELF-DISCIPLINE

- *Name the positive outcome first:* "You can go to the ball game as soon as you finish mowing the lawn."
- *Name the negative consequence second:* "But if you don't finish the lawn, you'll miss the game. When your ride comes, you'll have to explain that you can't go because you didn't finish your work."
- *Stay cool:* No yelling. No accusing. No predicting. No "I told you so." Just repeat the consequences and calmly carry them out.
- *Be ready to lose some free time:* You might have to change your own plans and stay home with your teen if he misses the ball game. You'll also need to monitor your teen's room to be sure he doesn't sneak out, and you'll have to stay nearby until he finishes the lawn. A little inconvenience now will prevent a ton of agony later.

We succeed in life when we have mastered the necessary skills. Before you go backpacking, for instance, you must buy certain equipment, pack certain supplies, and practice certain skills. Without all this up-front action, your good intentions won't keep the bugs off, the rain out, or your hunger satisfied. As your teenager hikes through life, give her the equipment and skills she needs to complete the adventure safely. These skills go way beyond getting homework done on time.

The process of skill training, however, doesn't come easily or naturally. For parents, monitoring is the hard part. But choosing to supervise homework, chores, and attitudes is like giving your teen a safety harness. Work before pleasure keeps your teen from falling into the abyss of never accomplishing anything, which leads to the crash landing of feeling like a failure. Breaking big projects down into small ones keeps your teen from falling into despair, which crashes into so much pressure that she's immobilized.

Household chores are as important as schoolwork. Chore training includes showing a teen how to actually clean a commode or scrub a bathtub, showing where to dump the grass clippings, inspecting for quality control, and timing how long each job takes so adequate time can be allotted in the future. Homework, chores, relating well to others, all of these build a teenager's confidence and prepare him to succeed as an independent adult.

MEANWHILE, BACK AT JESSIE'S HOUSE...

On Saturday, Jessie rolled out of bed about eleven o'clock. The phone rang fifteen minutes later, and she ran to answer it.

"Whoa, Jessie. No talking on the phone until you finish those chapters and study for that test."

"But, Dad!" Jessie cried, panic in her voice. "The caller ID says it's

Ben. He promised to call, and I waited all day yesterday. I *have* to talk to him."

"Let the machine get it. Then after we've gone over the chapters and test material, you can call him back."

"You are so unfair!"

"I know. I took a refresher course on parenting, and I got straight A's in unfair."

"That's for sure!" Jessie stomped off to find her books.

CONTROL OR GUIDANCE?

Parents might resist such concentrated supervision of their teenagers. If you're worried about turning into a control freak, consider the reasons you, as a parent, need to guide the process of teaching life skills:

- Control works things out for your own convenience, while guidance shows your teen how to organize life for her own welfare.
- Control says, "Do it because I say so," while guidance says, "Do it because it's the right thing to do."
- Control says, "I'm the only one who can choose well," while guidance says, "Which action and attitude can you choose that will best honor God?"
- Control says, "I'm the center of the universe," while guidance says, "What will help all of us work together as a family?"
- Control says, "I want to look good in front of my friends," while guidance says, "I want *you* to look good and to do the right thing in front of your friends."
- Control says, "I want to succeed through you," while guidance says, "I want *you* to succeed. Here's how."

Her dad picked up the cordless phone to keep with him. Otherwise, it might be too great a temptation for his daughter.

"Where's my phone?" Jessie hollered a few minutes later.

"I have it out here. As soon as the chapters and test are studied, you can have it back."

"Ohhh! You know I can't study when I'm mad!"

"I guess you'll have to find a way. And don't forget that the report has to be written before you go out tonight."

Things remained quiet for forty-five minutes, then Jessie emerged from her room. Her eyes still held a bit of fire, but she was ready to be quizzed. She knew the chapters well, but her dad sent her back to study more completely for her math test. She complained again but returned to her desk. Thirty minutes later, she knew the material well.

"Now can I call Ben?"

"Sure. Just keep in mind how long the report will take. Set your watch so you won't talk for too long."

"But, Dad, you've always told me that people matter more than tasks!"

"Yes, that's true. But the tasks still have to be completed. It's called balancing life."

"Aren't you a fountain of wisdom today!"

"Whoa. Say that again, but with respect."

Jessie repeats her statement with exaggerated sweetness. Her dad thanks her and off she goes. She then calls Ben and talks for more than an hour. Her dad wonders if she's leaving enough time to finish her paper.

Soon she comes out of her room all glowy eyed, obviously charmed by the dashing Ben. "Daddy! (she uses that endearment only when she's deliriously happy) Ben asked to drive me to the party. Can you believe it? This is a dream come true!"

"You've waited for this for a long time! If he weren't a guy, I'd be happy too!"

"Oh, Daddy, there *are* nice guys," Jessie contends. "They're not all bad!"

"Well, maybe. Now hurry and get that report written!"

"Dad, you're not going to hold me to that with Ben picking me up in three hours, are you?"

Jessie's a real charmer, and she nearly wins her dad over. But he stands his ground. "I'm afraid the rules still apply. You knew yesterday that the paper had to be done by tonight. You chose to relax yesterday afternoon, and you slept late today. Nothing wrong with those things, except that it didn't leave much time for spontaneous surprises."

"Spontaneous surprises?"

"Yes, like Ben driving you to the party."

"But, Dad, it's Ben!"

"If you don't get moving, you'll be calling Ben and saying, 'Come later.'"

Jessie hurries off, fussing at her brother to get off the computer. Her dad calls for good manners, and two hours later Jessie hands over a draft of her report. It's amazingly strong for just over two hour's work. Her dad circles some spelling errors and hands it back.

"Now, Dad, *please* can I finish the paper tomorrow?"

He gives it some thought. "You at least have to make the spelling corrections and add a few revisions. Then print it out. You can give it a final read and reprint it tomorrow afternoon."

"Oh, Daddy, you're the best!" Jessie says with a hug. "But I have to start getting ready right now or I won't make it by the time Ben gets here."

"Call Ben and ask if he can come thirty minutes later. Didn't you say it was a drop-in party?"

"You can't be serious!"

"I'm very serious. You can tell him that your dad is making you finish your report first."

Jessie decides not to call Ben, thinking she could still get ready by the time he's due to arrive. Her dad notices her making the corrections haphazardly, so he reminds her to slow down or she'll have to revise it twice. She becomes more deliberate, finishes, hits "print," and jumps into the shower. Amazingly, she's ready within five minutes of Ben's arrival.

KEEP PRACTICING THE SKILL

Your teenager won't hug you for forcing her to complete homework assignments. She'll be absolutely convinced that you're destroying her friendships, making her a social outcast, and ruining her love life. She'll accuse you of being a control freak. She'll bring up all the times you don't get your own tasks done on time. But by persistently putting work before pleasure, you will be showing her that she can have friends and complete her homework, that she can have parties and persist through projects, that she can have a boyfriend and keep up with her home chores. It is possible to blend the easy and hard of life to get both done excellently.

But what if you set up a workable schedule and she still doesn't get her schoolwork finished before her date arrives at the door? This isn't a time to back down. You'll have to stand with her while she explains that she can't leave the house until she finishes revising her report. You might have to entertain the date while your teen keeps working. Or you might have to ask the suitor to come back in an hour.

Now think about another scenario. What if your teen has been waiting for this date for weeks, and she claims to go to her room to finish the paper. But instead, she sneaks out to meet her date just around the corner? If you suspect that type of evasion, you'll need to check on her. If she's missing, you'll drive to the party, escort her out, and bring her home to finish her paper. She'll make a scene, but your job is to help her build the life skills she needs, not to guarantee that she enjoys a party. Next weekend you'll repeat the whole homework-guiding process again so that eventually your teenager will follow through with only occasional checks from you.

MY TEEN REALLY STRUGGLES WITH SCHOOL

How should you handle things if your teenager must work around a learning disability, ADD, or ADHD? The principles in this chapter become even more important because they supply the structure, dependability, and strategies that make it possible for your teen to learn just like every other teen. You might also need to:

- Learn more about your teenager's particular challenge and how to manage it. A teen with a learning disability insists that LD does not mean "can't learn"; it means "learns differently." So talk to professionals and parents, do some research, and ask questions until you find the technology and strategies that will enable your teen to learn the material.

- Assure your teen that everybody faces challenges. "We will find a way around this."

- Sit with your teenager while she does her homework. Sometimes all she needs to maintain her focus is your presence. Other times she needs specific help.

- Set the times for homework so that your teen is especially well rested.

- When you're establishing deadlines, set a narrower choosing range, such as "show me your work within two hours" rather than "by tomorrow."

Teaching self-discipline is as hard for parents as learning the skill is difficult for teenagers. But it's entirely necessary. If teens could learn responsible behavior on their own, God wouldn't have designed families. Certainly in Bible times, some thirteen- and fourteen-year-olds took on adult responsibilities. But they had been taught to do so and had practiced those skills before launching out on their own. Experience, not a birthday, gives a person the ability to take on adult responsibility.

Our culture expands the length of time that adolescents depend on their parents, which adds a new level of tension. But it gives us the gift of more time to parent well. Our culture also adds the confusing dynamic of freedom combined with no responsibility. One expensive example is a car that belongs to the teenager but the parents pay for. Parents cover all the expenses and then wonder why their teens won't care for the car or won't get a job.

These trends make it more complex to parent teenagers. But our God can and does equip us for the challenge. We can let our teens drive one of our cars, an older one, rather than give them a late-model car on their sixteenth birthday. We can keep tying responsibility to freedom so our teens discover just how to be true adults. We can provide the tools for finishing tasks well: boundaries, study skills, timetables, the suggestion to listen to music while doing household chores, or whatever will help them accomplish the task.

Don't yell. Your teen will just yell back.

Don't nag. Your teen will just tune you out.

Simply supply the salt: Calmly explain the rewards for finishing and the unhappy consequences for not finishing. Then enforce those consequences no matter how inconvenient it becomes for you or how your teen reacts.

There will be emotional scenes. Your teen will yell, cry, storm off to her room. She will most definitely protest repeatedly and in a variety of ways (see more on this in chapter 10). But as you follow through, your teen will discover that once Dad or Mom says it, she'd better find a way to get it done. Each time your teenager succeeds at mastering a task, she ends up with more time. She grows more secure. She cultivates a necessary life skill. And peace reigns in your home.

Your teenager's happiness and success in adult life will grow from these years of guidance. It's easily worth all the effort—for you *and* for your teen.

ACTION STEPS

Your teen needs certain tools to succeed in life: time management, focusing skills, commitment to getting the hard stuff done no matter how distasteful, and good work habits. Making her do her homework and finish her chores gives her practice in using such tools. Without these life skills, even the most loving Christian teenager will create pain for others, and ultimately for herself.

What Scripture says: "There is a time for everything, and a season for every activity under heaven" (Ecclesiastes 3:1).

Explain to your teen: "When you do your homework first (or whatever the distasteful task), you can reward yourself later with free time. It's easy to pull yourself toward freedom; it's not easy to stop freedom so you can get to work. So put things in the order that will help assure they'll all get done."

5

MY TEEN *KNOWS* BETTER;

WHY WON'T HE *ACT* BETTER?

HELP YOUR TEENAGER OBEY
FROM THE HEART

Maia is stunned and heartsick. She logged on to the Internet to do some research, and while scanning the list of recently visited sites, she noticed several porn sites. The only two people who use this computer are Maia and her son, Jared. Why has he started checking out porn sites on the Internet? He knows better than that.

Uncertain exactly how to proceed, Maia decided to face this quandary head-on:

"Jared, I have something uncomfortable we need to talk about. While scanning recently visited sites to find the research site I used yesterday, I found that you had been visiting porn sites on the Internet."

"I *promise* I won't look at those sites anymore," Jared interrupted, absolutely mortified that his mom would bring up such a topic.

"I imagine you're as embarrassed as I am. But we have to talk about this because it's important to your happiness. When I noticed that you had gone to those sites on the Internet, I wanted to just ban you from the computer and pretend nothing had ever happened. But I'd rather give you some boundaries."

"Don't you trust me?" Jared couldn't believe his mother was doing this. "I know how to monitor myself!"

"Of course I trust you. I trust that you want to do the right thing. I also know that even grownups need structures to help us do the right thing—traffic tickets for speeding, penalties for not filing taxes on time, and more—so I'm going to give you those structures."

"It feels like you're putting me in prison!"

It was time to lighten the mood. "Even prisoners can earn privileges," Maia said lightly. "You might get extra bread and water for good behavior!"

Jared smiled in spite of himself, then hid the smile with a scowl. "So what are the rules?"

"You can only get online when Dad or I are home and awake. If you know we might walk in, you'll have a stronger motivation to stay away from bad sites."

"That's it?" Jared asked, amazed. Maia wondered if he had already thought of a way around that rule.

"That's the first rule. There are three. The second is that every night, with you standing next to me, I'll open the site history to see what sites have been visited. If any of them look suspicious, I'll go to them with you standing right there."

"There won't be any bad ones."

"That's what I'm counting on."

Every fiber in Maia's being wanted to stop right there. She wondered if she had been too harsh. But she kept going for the sake of her son. "I believe you when you say you'll stop visiting those sites. But there is more. I also want you to understand the principles. I want you to know the real truth about girls, to keep fake facts from blocking your fun."

"I told you, Mom. I won't look at those sites anymore!" insisted Jared.

"I believe you, Jared. But there are too many other sources of temptation, too many other places to find images of unhealthy sexual situations and photos of naked or barely clothed women. Ads and catalogs for some clothing stores are full of women posing in lingerie and skimpy underwear."

"Mom!"

"I'm not trying to embarrass you. In fact, I'm trying to affirm you for being attracted to the right things. The reason those photos appeal to you is that women are important. Your attraction to them is something God gave you."

"So it's all right to look at girls?"

"As long as they have clothes on, and as long as you see them as people, not as objects to stimulate your sexual urges."

"Are you sure?" Jared asked. "I thought every time I looked at a girl I had a dirty mind."

"There's nothing bad or dirty about being attracted to women. God created that attraction. In Genesis it says Adam and Eve were naked and not ashamed," Maia explained, convinced there was no way that she could continue this conversation much longer.

"Then why is it bad to look at the pictures on the Internet?"

"You're not married to those women. Nakedness is meant only for marriage. When you marry, you and your wife can be naked and not ashamed. Until marriage, though, you should feel a bit ashamed when you look at a woman's naked body."

"But you just said I'm not bad or dirty minded. Why is the human body something to be ashamed of?"

"God created our bodies to be shared within families. When you were young, I bathed you and dressed you. Now you do that yourself and you don't want me walking into the bathroom when you're in there. One day you'll be ready to share your body with your wife. Until then, your body is not to be looked at or touched by anyone but the woman you will marry."

"Mom!"

"I know. I know. I'm being a totally embarrassing mom. But we're just talking privately. Part of the reason it's embarrassing is because it's so important. I know looking at these images is exciting, but believe me, it will damage your relationships with women in years to come. This is too important not to talk about."

"But I'm not touching anybody. What's so wrong about just looking and imagining?"

"Sharing bodies is part of intimacy. Looking is the first step. When you look, you begin to think about what it would be like to be close to the person. The steps of looking and thinking are parts of a precious process and not meant to be isolated from marriage. They get twisted when we detach them from a committed, lifelong relationship. God designed looking and thinking to be tied to knowing the person— what she believes, dreams of, and seeks to achieve in life."

"You're losing me, Mom."

"What I'm trying to say is the only scantily clothed woman you should look at is the one you're married to. Looking at other women betrays the command of God in Philippians 4:8: 'Whatever is true, whatever is noble, whatever is right, whatever is pure, whatever is lovely, whatever is admirable—if anything is excellent or praiseworthy—think about such things.'"

"But you just said it's good to like women. So aren't I being true, noble, right, pure, and all that when I admire a woman?"

"It's only true, noble, and those other things when you look and love within the commitment of marriage," Maia explained.

"So what do I do until then? Just close my eyes?"

"Actually that's exactly what you need to do."

IMITATE GOD'S LOVE AND GUIDANCE

When I talk to parents about helping their teens resist ungodly influences, some question the appropriateness of hands-on direction with a teenager.

"Won't that take away my teen's heart obedience?" they argue. "Isn't a teen supposed to monitor himself? Aren't morality and obedience to God supposed to come from the heart, not from some external pressure?"

Yes, eventually. To discover why direct guidance of teens is appropriate, notice the way God guides us adults into right actions and attitudes. He shows us the truth; he explains the consequences; then he expects us to obey him, period, no matter how we feel, no matter how great the temptation, no matter how many other people are refusing to do what's right. He even promises us a way of escape when the temptation seems overwhelming (see 1 Corinthians 10:13). Quite often, for teenagers, that way of escape is parental supervision. Maia wisely gave her son this supervision:

"I told you there were three rules. The third rule is that I have the right to check your room for any books or magazines you're reading."

"You can't do that! It's my stuff!" Jared countered. Then he quickly added, "Not that I would hide anything."

"If you know your stuff will be seen, you'll more likely choose good reading material. If you know you can hide it, you might sneak something in that's inappropriate."

"But it's *my* stuff!"

"Yes it is. And you're my responsibility."

Jared has three rules. His acts of obedience to his parents and to God are valid because he obeys those rules, not because he *feels like* obeying (see James 2:15-16; Matthew 7:21-27). God does not say, "Obey me only when your heart feels like it." He wants us to obey even when we don't feel like it. In the Old Testament, God gave his chosen people the Law, which could be summed up as "obey me or face bad results." Then came the New Testament, in which he stressed the will of our heart over outward adherence to the Law. Though heart obedience is preferable, the heart first must be trained. Heart obedience doesn't come about on its own. It grows out of a direct experience with living according to God's truth. Parents are a key to helping this happen. Because Jared's mom cares enough to teach him about women, he will have experience in managing his manly yearnings. After he has obeyed the rules long enough, he will understand God's purposes for him as a man. He can then monitor himself and set his own boundaries. His obedience will come from the heart.

Until then, however, Maia must give him practice obeying good rules.

GIVE REASONS FOR WHAT YOU ASK

When it comes to a habit such as viewing pornography, theology is well and good. But your teen must also know how to apply that theology. What Jared needs is a strategy that will enable him to avoid the trap of adult Internet sites. Maia considered the simplest solution: Pull the plug on the computer. That might stop the problem for a time, but it will crop up again.

Inappropriate sexual material is everywhere—online, in print, in music, on billboards, in movies—so Maia must teach her teen to manage it wisely. If not, the world's ungodly influences will manage him. If the parents in the Sleeping Beauty fairy tale had taught their daughter about spinning wheels rather than hide them from her, she would not have been dangerously curious when she discovered one. In a similar way, your son is curious about women and your daughters are curious about men, and rightly so. So teach them how to satisfy that curiosity in healthy ways.

Teach your teens how to relate to members of the opposite sex in ways that are positive and mutually enriching—for themselves, for the people they date, and for their future spouses. Here's how Maia started the process:

"The only way to manage the temptation to look at images of

naked women is to shut yourself off from the images. Turn off the television when a sex scene comes on, exit immediately if you accidentally land on a pornographic Web site, leave if you're at a friend's house and he pulls out certain magazines or videos."

"Yeah, right, Mom. What am I going to say when they say, 'A little look won't hurt. What's the matter? Don't you like girls?'"

"You'll say, 'Of course I like girls. It's just that I prefer waiting until I can look at the girl I'm married to.'"

"Yeah—and get laughed off the block."

"Maybe. But more likely they'll think it's no big deal when you give some casual reason to leave like, 'Well guys. I hate to go, but I just remembered an assignment I have.' Your assignment could be homework or mowing the lawn or even the assignment from God to keep your eyes from viewing evil."

"Mom, you keep going back and forth. First you say it's evil to look at girls. Then you say it's a good gift from God. Would you make up your mind?"

"I know it sounds confusing. Think about ice cream. It's a good and satisfying treat. But if you take it out of the freezer and put it in the sun, the taste and texture melt into a yucky mess. The dessert you were looking forward to is now a disgusting sight. You'd never consider it a treat. It's the same with sex. God created sexuality to be a good and satisfying treat. But when you take it out of marriage it degrades so that no matter how many pictures you look at, you're never satisfied, never happy. That kind of sexual excitement can never be fulfilling."

"But you're not a guy. You don't know how hard it is!"

"You're right. I'm not a guy. But I'm not a thief or a murderer either. And I don't have to be in their shoes to know that robbing and killing hurt other people."

"Yeah, but looking at pictures doesn't hurt anyone. I'm just looking. I'm not committing adultery. I'm just looking."

"Thieves would say that what they do is harmless as well. 'It's just one small item. The store won't miss it.' So they take the CD or game cartridge and experience that heady feeling of power that comes when you get away with something that's forbidden. At first, all they wanted was the item they stole, but the surprising rush of power makes them want to try it again. Only next time, they steal something bigger. Looking at pornography is like that. The initial thrill is bigger than you expected, so you want more explicitness next time to maintain the level of excitement."

"That happens to perverts. Not to me."

"You may be right. But most perverts start out as regular guys with a healthy curiosity. Because you're a full-blooded male, women already fascinate you. That's as it should be. But don't make that interest even harder to manage. Looking at certain pictures makes the intrigue stronger in an unhealthy way. Because pictures can't provide the personal interaction that a relationship does, you get more and more frustrated and look for more and more pictures. The problem is that they will never satisfy. Pornography creates unnecessary frustration, and I don't want you going through that pain."

Maia went on to explain that looking at pornography is more than mere curiosity; it's tied in with a teen's fantasy life. Looking at sex-oriented videos or images on the Internet feeds lust, which for hormonally charged boys leads quickly to masturbation. When Jared argues that "it's only looking," he's telling only part of the story. Pornography takes normal curiosity and channels it into lust. Looking at pornography can create all sorts of problems later on when a teen marries the girl of his dreams and finds that she's nothing like the over-sexed fantasy girl portrayed on the Internet site.

"I just wish you'd trust me," Jared told his mom. "I don't go to the hard-core sites. It's just photos. I'm not hurting anybody."

"Even looking is to be saved for marriage. We've got to trust God that even if we don't recognize the bad effects, looking still hurts you."

Jared is not convinced. But that doesn't mean he won't become convinced later. And whether Jared acts hesitant or cooperative at this point, Maia knows not to back down. She must keep the three rules in place: no site searching on Jared's part, checking the sites every night with Jared present, and her checking his room at random intervals. Remember: Your goal is to teach your teens to relate to real live people rather than get their information from magazines or the computer. Show your daughters and sons how to like themselves so others will like them and treat them with respect. Explain how both sons and daughters can dress and carry themselves in ways that respect God, themselves, and the ones they want to date. Pornography is based on the exploitation of the viewer's lustful impulses. It has no regard for the dignity of the individuals being portrayed or for those who view the pornography. Avoiding such material builds respect for the young people our teens date, making it easier to treat them with honor as God's creations, and not as the object of lustful desire.

While teenage girls typically don't gravitate to Internet images of nude men, they are heavily influenced by the media's obsession with skin-baring fashion. Girls are led to believe that boys won't pay attention to them unless they dress in tight-fitting and revealing clothing. We need to teach our daughters how to relate well to guys, how to have a healthy view of themselves as women, and how to dress and carry themselves in a way that shows respect for themselves and for God.

WON'T HE JUST OUTGROW IT?

A heightened curiosity about women and sex is normal among teenage boys. But pornographers, motivated by financial gain, are quick to exploit your teenager's raging hormones and powerful sexual impulses. Temptations and dangers are plentiful, so God has commissioned parents to show teens the way to go. Whether it's sexual immorality or disrespectful speech or some other destructive behavior, start working in concert with God to provide focused guidance. When the Bible says to train up a child in the way he should go, it doesn't mean to just take him to church or to just talk about right and wrong. It means to actually show our teens *how* to do the right thing and then to make certain they do it. Just as job training involves instruction, demonstration, and review, so training our teenagers in righteousness requires our focused involvement. Here are some ways to do this:

- *Refusal to obey the first time.* Your teen must learn to honorably obey legitimate authority figures. As he obeys you, even when he disagrees, he'll learn to obey God. *Solution:* Consistently provide uncomfortable consequences for disobedience as well as comfortable consequences and increased freedoms for good behavior.

- *Playing one parent against another.* This is a form of refusing to obey: Dad won't let me go to the party, so I'll talk Mom into letting me go. *Solution:* Even if you and your spouse disagree on a rule, restriction, or decision, stand united in front of your kids. Then talk privately about any changes that need to be made.

- *Acting or speaking in cruel ways to siblings.* Family harmony is essential; cruelty is destructive. So act quickly to put a stop to unkindness and disrespect. *Solution:* Insist on kind words and intervene immediately when mean or cutting words are used. Don't believe the myth that it's normal for siblings to be cruel to each other. Refusing to address this habit saddles your younger children with the suspicion that maybe they really are as stupid as big brother says they are. It also communicates that it's okay to abuse others with words as long as you're bigger or as long as you abuse a family member.

- *Selfishness and self-centeredness.* We're all born thinking we're the center of the universe. Unless you teach your teen otherwise, he'll expect to always be happy, always have things go his way, and always be able to talk his way out of trouble. *Solution:* Prod him to stop and consider what's good for others, not just what works to his own benefit (see Philippians 2:3-4).

- *Lack of direction.* Dreamers who don't act on their plans are desperately unhappy people. They never make progress toward achieving their dreams, and they often assume that if they just dream another dream things will be fine. *Solutions:* Each time your teen has a dream, show her how to take significant steps toward achieving that dream—save up money from odd jobs to buy that stereo, shadow someone in an interesting career field, push on through to gain that next level of skill in music or sports.

- *Drug use.* This potentially life-threatening pattern originates with the failure to move past selfishness or lack of direction. When parents cater to their teens' whims, the teens begin to believe that life should always work out in their favor. But when they hit the real world of school and friends and sports, they find that things often *don't* go their way, so they try to create a place where they always feel good. That's why teaching a mature view of self and others can help prevent drug abuse. *Solutions:* Work toward obedience even when it's inconvenient, respect for others even if you disagree with them, and selfless persistence in working toward goals. When teens learn at home that the universe doesn't revolve around them, they will be able to handle real life without the aid of drugs.

No, your teens won't just outgrow bad behaviors any more than the plants in a garden can ward off weeds. God has given you the responsibility to mold your teens. You stake plants so they'll grow straight, weave vines so they'll climb a trellis, reinforce the branches of a sapling so they won't break before they can grow strong. The same principles apply to your teenaged son or daughter. Matthew 12:33 urges us to "Make a tree good and its fruit will be good." What's inside a person will become evident in the person's life and will be demonstrated through words and actions (see Matthew 12:34-35).

As you stake, reinforce, and weave your teenager's morality, love as God loves. God loves us with a never-ending love as he shows us what to do and why. Maia's son, Jared, who had been accessing immoral Web sites, needed his mom to teach him not only what God's rules are regarding sexual purity, but also how those rules work to protect him from harm. Then he needed some boundaries that would make certain he obeyed the rules.

In working with your teen on rules and boundaries, mirror the consistency of Christ, who is "the same yesterday and today and forever" (Hebrews 13:8). Heart and Law were both present in the Old Testament, just as they were present in New Testament times and today. Through Christ, God the Father showed his heart of love toward us, and through Christ, we can live in heart obedience to the Father. Just as God does through Christ, expect and enforce obedience even when your teen doesn't feel like obeying. Then your teen will develop habits of obedience.

Remember, teens will manage to grow out of very few bad behaviors on their own. Habits have power, and habits formed during adolescence will exert a grip on your son or daughter well past the teen years—for better or for worse. If you have trouble following through on enforcing rules, ask your spouse or a close friend to hold you accountable. Together you can do it.

Whether motivated by heart or rules, teens show love for God by choosing the right action. Don't fall for the lie that if you let your kids do wrong they will eventually come around to an inner motivation to do what's right. Doing wrong can harden them to God and blind them to his leading. Equally powerful, doing right softens teens' hearts toward God. Insisting that our teens do right orients them toward God and his will. Every day our teens are involved in a spiritual battle; the worst thing we can do is send them off without making sure they are trained and prepared. Army recruits don't go through basic training because they love the discipline, but because it will prepare them to triumph on the field of battle.

TALK ABOUT IT

How can teenagers have positive relationships with the opposite sex? Good views about their own bodies? We've discussed it from a teenage

---

LIFE HABITS TO GROW

A choice that is repeated enough times becomes a pattern. That pattern repeated becomes a habit. That habit repeated becomes a lifestyle. Guiding your teen's habits is more than stopping the bad ones; it's also starting the good ones. Spend time thinking how you will help your teenager grow each of these essential life habits:
- Speak kindly and directly rather than attacking others with words.
- Refuse to let mood or fatigue serve as excuses for grumpy behavior.
- Allow parents to finish speaking before replying.
- Turn off the computer, close the book, or change the television channel when people are depicted using or abusing others. (Your ultimate goal is to prompt your teen to monitor himself.)
- Treat each person with kindness and respect, just as you want them to treat you.

boy's point of view and then adapted the same principles for teenage girls. Affirm your son's natural interest in women and their bodies. Curiosity about women, and an attraction to the female form, are normal (as it is normal for girls to be attracted to guys). So agree with your son that, yes, pictures of naked women are interesting and appealing. God made us to be attracted to the opposite sex. But looking at images of naked people and sexual situations on the Internet is not a healthy or God-honoring way to satisfy this legitimate curiosity.

If you're a mom with a teenage son, this talk could be uncomfortable. Even some dads resist the idea of such a frank talk about pornography. But remember, sons will be embarrassed too, even when talking to Dad. They'll give plenty of eye rolling and declarations that they already know all they need to know about sex. But don't put off discussions like these (it's more than just THE talk), thinking that it would be easier to just leave things alone. If you don't teach your teen about

---

NIP IT IN THE BUD

Guiding your teenagers to virtuous behavior doesn't have to be long and ponderous. Use a few single-line explanations delivered with seriousness but no shame:

- Teen: "You just don't understand!" Parent: "Understanding is not the issue here. Good behavior is."
- Teen: "Well, I'm not going to do what you say." Parent: "It's your choice. But if you ever want to leave your room again, I'd choose to cooperate."
- Teen: "That's not fair." Parent: "Actually it is. Everyone must do the right thing or suffer the consequences."
- Teen: "You can't make me." Parent: "You're exactly right. Only you can do that. My job is to make the consequences so severe that you'll want to make yourself do the right thing."

---

real love, plenty of other people will step in to teach him their own form of destructive sexuality. Keep your teen from being used and abused by vaccinating him with the truth. A bit of embarrassment now will save him, his girlfriends, and his future wife a lot of pain.

HELP YOUR TEEN FOLLOW THROUGH

Most parents do really well at telling their kids what to do and not do. A huge proportion of these parents also add good reasons for their rules. But only a precious few make certain their teens follow through in carrying out that right behavior.

Why?

Because it's hard. It takes time and creativity, and it requires confrontation. So why follow through? Explaining the whats and whys of right behavior won't do a bit of good if you don't give your teen the boundaries and the consequences that will motivate choosing the right attitudes and actions. Jesus told a parable about a father who approached his sons with a request. The first son said he would not obey but then changed his mind and did the right thing. The second son agreed to obey but never followed through. After telling the parable, Jesus helped the religious leaders of Jerusalem understand that the son who paid lip service was not the one who did his father's will. The first son, the one who initially resisted his father's request but then changed his mind, was the obedient son (see Matthew 21:28-31). Obeying God is the right thing to do, no matter how we arrive at our decision to obey. It can be motivated by rules, boundaries, consequences, or heart motivation. So as you talk to your teen, go ahead and put some safety measures into place. Here is how Maia handled it with Jared:

"Son, I've tried to explain some of the reasons why looking at provocative pictures of women or sexually explicit situations is wrong. I have to put some boundaries in place to help you resist that temptation. God does this for us. He shows us the reason to do and not do certain things. Then he puts rules into place and expects us to obey them whether we agree with the reasons or not. As we understand the reasons, he invites us to put our own rules into place. So when you're ready, I want you to add your rules to mine."

PUT GOOD BOUNDARIES IN PLACE

Once Maia listed the new rules, her son was mad as a snake, and things were tense every time she looked over the nightly Internet history. But she must follow through. She is investing in his future success in relationships with girls and ultimately in his marriage. If she doesn't intervene now, she risks his addiction to pornography. She also risks a very unhappy marriage for him. Many men who abuse women and children trace their habits all the way back to a few peeks at pornography when

---

WHY CAN'T YOU BE COOL LIKE EVERYBODY ELSE'S MOM?

To build your teen's trust in talking with you about hard subjects, put together some principles of parental weirdness. Samples:

- When you're a teenager, almost everything your parent does is embarrassing.
- Other parents can do embarrassing things, but you think they're funny. Why? You don't have to worry that people will associate you with their silly actions.
- Other people's mothers seem cooler because they aren't the ones telling you to get to bed on time, correcting your actions, and making you do chores. In fact, you probably like cleaning up after parties over there because nobody forces you. It's different when you're at home.

---

they were young. One peek led to a compulsion that grew into abusing others.

Staying on top of the situation won't come easily for Maia or for you. You'll come up with plenty of reasons not to follow through on the rules you set. If you think hard enough, in fact, you can easily rationalize a course of nonintervention:

- He's home after school by himself, so there's no way I can supervise him. (*Rationalization:* You're allowing just two hours of the day to excuse you from supervising the other twenty-two hours.)
- She's gonna be out on her own before long anyway, and then I won't be able to do anything. (*Rationalization:* Since my daughter will leave for college in two years, I have an excuse for being lazy now.)
- He's got to learn from his mistakes. (*Rationalization:* If he burns his hand on a hot stove, he'll learn without my having to monitor his behavior all the time.)
- If I enforce a rule that's this strict, I'll set him up for lying to me. (*Rationalization:* I'm not willing to spend the time it will take to check his homework, his chores, and his use of the computer to see if he's telling the truth about following the rules.)

Each of these rationalizations underscores an equally powerful reason to follow through, no matter how much time and effort it requires:

- He's home after school by himself, and I have no control over what he does then. (*Reason for rules:* If I supervise him well for the twenty-two hours I am available to him, he just might manage the two independent hours on his own.)
- She's gonna be out on her own before long, and then she won't be around to be supervised. (*Reason for rules:* So I need to make the most of the little time we have. If I guide her well while she's at home, she'll understand the how and why of choosing

well, rather than experiment with danger when she's an independent young adult.)

- He's got to learn from his mistakes. (*Reason for rules:* The harder
  he argues against the rules, the more scared he really is. Plus,
  some mistakes are deadly. If he could see the bigger picture, he
  wouldn't need parents.)
- If I enforce a rule that's this strict, I'll set him up for lying to
  me. (*Reason for rules:* If he lies to me, that's a problem all its
  own. If I see evidence of lying, we'll deal with it as a separate
  matter. But rather than assume he's lying, I'll explain that I
  want to catch him doing the right thing, not the wrong thing.)

God has arranged the world in such a way to make it possible for
us to find and build good relationships. If we attempt to work outside
those boundaries, we will create pain for ourselves. Choose to structure
your home in the same ways—with bumper walls of safety so your teen
knows what to do and why. Then he can grow patterns of choosing
that enable him to treat himself and others with dignity, to build a good
marriage based on respecting his wife, and to honor God with his life.

INVITE TALK ABOUT WHY
GOOD ACTIONS WORK

Finally, and perhaps hardest of all, check with your teen after a time to
see how things are going. When he can voice how a positive life habit is
impacting him well, he will more likely adopt that life habit as his own.
This is your goal—that all the rules and boundaries and checking up
will lead to a positive and self-motivated habit. You'll know that has
happened when you hear your teenager say, "I was watching a late movie
the other night, and a bunch of stuff came on that dishonored women.
I just couldn't stand seeing girls treated that way, so I turned it off."

Even when he doesn't bring it up, ask questions like, "Son, how are things going in managing visual temptation? What other temptations have reared their ugly heads? What still bugs you that I might help you with?"

He might say, "I figured out that I wouldn't want anyone looking at my sister the way guys look at the models in magazines. Those girls are somebody's sisters. So I want to respect all women like I'd want them to respect my sister."

Or your son may say nothing at all.

And even if he says the right things, he might still be doing the wrong things. So keep supervising. And keep listening. Through supervising and listening, you show that you trust your teen to assess situations and choose good behavior.

As you find evidence that your son is monitoring himself well, back off of daily checking, but still check regularly and randomly. Keep checking the computer, watching his room and backpack, paying attention to what he does and where he goes. If you find evidence that he has been accessing pornography, step up the checkpoints.

All the way through, thank him each time you see him monitoring himself well: "Son, you're showing true signs of manhood by choosing what you see and don't see. Any kid can let pornography pull him in. You're acting like a true man with a real heart."

IT'S A FEMALE ISSUE TOO

Though pornography is by and large a male problem, it does tempt girls as well. Look at today's fashions. The emphasis is on accentuating body parts that are traditionally kept covered. Girls know that guys respond when they see a bare midriff or exposed cleavage or curves accentuated by tight-fitting clothing. Because girls enjoy attention, your daughter might pressure you to allow her to dress in clothing that's fashionable but inappropriate. Don't give in.

God requires modesty in dress and behavior. Calling attention to ourselves for the wrong reasons is forbidden in the Bible, as is behavior or dress that would provoke lust. Explain to your daughter that she not only harms herself, but also the boys around her, when she dresses inappropriately. Explain to her that the attention such dress attracts isn't an interest in her as a person but in her as an object.

Whether you have a son or a daughter, your teen is facing unspoken temptation. It might be fantasy romance pursued in Internet chat rooms or other unhealthy ways of relating. Or it might be something entirely different, such as unkindness toward others, ruthless competition, gossip, materialism, or the desire just to give up and quit trying in

---

Not *My* Teenager!

Before you rule out the possibility that your son visits "adult" Web sites, note these disturbing statistics:

- A service that measures Internet activity discovered that 27.5 percent of minors (age seventeen and under) visited an adult site in a single month, representing more than 3,000,000 unique visitors. Compare this to only 802,400 minors who visited one of the most popular music sites.
- 21.2 percent of the minors visiting adult sites are age fourteen or younger.
- 40.2 percent of the visitors were female.
- At least some youth land on pornographic sites accidentally, due to links they don't initially recognize as being pornographic.

What to do? Teach your teens to exit immediately if they find themselves in an adult site and to tell you about such sites. This strategy gives your teen a branch to grasp so he won't suffocate in quicksand. (For more information about who uses the Internet and how they use it, see http://us.netvalue.com.)

---

school. Satan will custom design a temptation that caters to your teen's area of vulnerability. Whatever it is, good actions motivated by a parent's rules can lead to true heart obedience. As a parent who wants her teen to eventually develop heart obedience, you can apply these same principles, no matter what the obedience issue is.

- Imitate God in the way you invite obedience.
- Give reasons for what you're asking.
- Show how to do that good action.
- Follow through by placing and enforcing appropriate boundaries.
- Invite your teen to voice why that good action works.

ACTION STEPS

You really can legislate morality. As you insist on certain good behaviors and provide the boundaries for making certain your teen chooses those good behaviors, heart obedience will eventually follow. It's like providing training wheels so your teen can ride the bike of life without crashing.

What Scripture says: "Do not think that I have come to abolish the Law or the Prophets; I have not come to abolish them but to fulfill them" (Matthew 5:17).

Explain to your teen: "God doesn't say, 'Obey me when you feel like it.' Instead he expects us to do the right thing, period. Because God gives us rules to guide us to happiness, I'm going to do the same for you. I will also teach you why each rule works. Then I will give you boundaries that help you obey. My goal is that you will eventually choose to do it without the rule—that's heart obedience."

6

MY TEENAGER IS HEADED
FOR TROUBLE

TAKE DECISIVE ACTION BEFORE
YOUR TEEN RUINS HIS LIFE

Sam had always been a good kid, full of smiles and eager to help others. As a high school freshman, Sam joined FFA, an organization for students interested in farming and agribusiness. He even ran for vice president and won. Sam's parents never pictured him heading off to college to major in agriculture, but the kids in the group were courteous and a lot of fun to have around. They made Sam feel comfortable just being himself. So his parents stopped worrying and decided the group was doing their son a lot of good.

But Sam started worrying just about the time his parents stopped. More and more, kids at school were calling him a "hick" and a "kicker." At first he just ignored the taunting because he enjoyed being vice president of the FFA. He also enjoyed the new friends he had made in the organization. But after a year of ridicule, Sam decided he didn't want to be known as a hayseed. He pulled out of FFA and began to look for new friends.

As too often happens when a teen seeks out new friends, the search led to trouble. In this case, a boy with serious problems attached himself to Sam. Other kids, who would have been much better companions, were already busy with their own activities. Though they didn't mean to leave Sam out, they failed to notice that he was looking for a new crowd. They assumed he still had FFA activities on the weekends, as he had during the previous year when they invited him to do things.

While the solid kids were occupied with their own after-school activities, a troubled boy named Drew had no such involvements. He was a needy kid who was glad to claim Sam as a friend. Sam's parents hadn't met Drew, so they were rightly uneasy when he invited Sam to a party. Sam seemed delighted, so his parents said he could go. They were glad that, finally, someone was inviting Sam to do something.

The party turned out to be a kegger, and some of the kids brought marijuana. The goal of the party, as for most gatherings with alcohol, was to get drunk or high and to act as goofy as possible. Sam wasn't comfortable with drinking since his parents didn't keep alcohol in the house. And until that night he hadn't seen anyone smoke marijuana. But since these new friends seemed to like him, Sam decided that it wouldn't hurt to have just one beer. Maybe he could even witness to these guys.

Sam carried around the same cup of beer for most of the night, taking only small sips. When the party was over, he hadn't quite finished that one glass. He had passed the test with the other guys but was still clear-headed for the drive home. Although Drew bragged about holding his liquor, he had definitely had too many. Sam dropped his friend off and headed home with the car windows open to get rid of the alcohol smell. He was glad his parents were asleep when he came in. He gargled some mouthwash and crawled into bed.

The following weekend Sam went to another party at a different house, but with the same routine. Lots of raucous laughter and stories comparing how much each kid planned to drink. He was thankful that the marijuana smokers didn't show up, and he again carried around just one glass of beer all evening. He didn't like the taste of beer, but he didn't want to look stupid in front of the others.

As the school year progressed, one weekend with Drew followed another. Sam's parents still had not met Drew, and they wondered why Sam avoided bringing his friend by the house. But Sam insisted that he was meeting a lot of great kids through Drew, while carefully skirting around any details about the parties they went to.

Near the end of the first semester, at another party with Drew, Sam finished a full glass of beer. The taste was growing on him, and he never had any trouble driving home. Soon he was up to two drinks and still doing the driving. Meanwhile the warning signals were going off for Sam's parents. Drew hardly ever did things with Sam at the house, and Sam had developed a strange, hollow look in his eyes.

Finally they confronted their son, asking why Drew never came around and why Sam was doing all the driving. Sam shrugged off their inquiries. "Drew's dad always has the car, so he has no way to get around. That's why I volunteer to drive," he explained. "And I look tired because I've had a lot of tests to study for. Listen, I like my new friends. They're introducing me to more and more people, and they're good kids. There's nothing to worry about!"

Sam's parents pushed away their suspicions. *Maybe we're just being overly protective,* they reasoned. *After all, we've been praying that Sam would find some good friends.*

Then late one Friday night they received a call from the police telling them Sam had been in an accident. The two boys in the car escaped with only cuts and bruises, thanks to the airbags, but they ended up on opposite sides of a telephone pole. The car was totaled. Both boys had been drinking, so Sam had to stay at the police station until a parent picked him up and agreed to keep him home for forty-eight hours.

"This must be a mistake," Sam's dad told the officer. "It can't be my son. Sam doesn't drink." Then he added, "I'll be right there."

GOOD DECISION MAKING

A teenager is making decisions that will affect the rest of his life. So help your teen develop these wise habits before launching him into the world after high school:

Find people you want to be like. Because you will become like those you spend time with, choose to spend the most time with the friends you want to be like.

Run from temptation. None of us is "strong enough" to resist. The best defense is distance (see 1 Timothy 6:11).

Make your own choices. Look at all the options. Do you want to be on the academic decathlon team rather than the soccer team? Go for it!

Manage your own time. If you don't choose how to spend your days, someone else will decide for you. Once an hour is spent, you never get it back. So be careful in the use of your time.

Detach yourself from weak friends. No matter where you go, there are people who will use you or zap your strength. Politely stay away from people who have issues that keep them from giving as well as receiving in a friendship.

Seek out Christian fellowship. Do more than sit in church. Talk with and serve alongside other believers. Get involved!

Keep a good reputation. Once you compromise sexually, once you use drugs, or once you join an unhealthy group of friends, it's hard to regain a clean reputation. At the same time, don't let one mistake make you think you must slide down the slippery slope to further sin. Choose to turn around (see 1 John 1:9).

DIAGNOSE THE PROBLEM

The phone call from the police station was a wake-up call for Sam's parents. They are relieved that he wasn't injured, but they agonize over how this could have happened. They've always been a close Christian family. Sam has never seen his parents touch alcohol, except for a few champagne toasts at wedding receptions. When they think how close he came to being killed, they start to shake. Why has he taken this turn?

Sadly, Sam's dilemma is not unusual. Good kids get into bad situations, and though they try their best, they make wrong choices. Before they know it, they're in trouble and can't get themselves out. Some land in jail or in the morgue. In Sam's case, he began making bad decisions because there weren't enough anchors to keep him from drifting. He needed the anchor of his parents being awake when he came home so they could ask about the party, find out who else was there, and listen to his stories. Knowing that his parents would wait up for him and smell the alcohol could have anchored Sam to resist the sway of having "just one beer."

He also needed the anchor of his parents insisting on meeting Drew. They needed to follow through on their feelings of uneasiness, and they should have checked to see if the parties were supervised by adults. Any teenager can drift if his parents and other supportive adults don't give him enough anchors. Like Sam, many kids who make mistakes come from families that love and care about them. The families may have taught well, disciplined well, and modeled well. Or they may have talked a lot about loving guidance while failing to provide it. Either way, if your teen takes a wrong turn, don't get stuck looking backward. Glance back only long enough to learn from your blunders. Then move decisively forward.

No matter how bad the blunder, parents can always guide their teenagers back to the right path. The key is to step up the care when mistakes happen. Sam saw just enough examples of drinking-to-have-fun at wedding receptions that he chose to try that path with his new group of friends. He also turned his back on solid friends to become part of what he perceived to be a cooler crowd. And he had no parental assistance to help him walk the tightrope back to good friends. But that is all in the past. The important thing now is how his parents handle his unwise choice of companions and his decision to drink. The failure to take decisive action will have serious consequences later on.

Katie's parents found this out the hard way. The first time she was arrested for shoplifting, they paid her court costs and requested that the judge remove it from her record. The second time, they did the same and gave their daughter a lengthy lecture. The third time they didn't even find out about Katie's string of thefts until they saw it in the newspaper. Eventually Katie landed a jail sentence. Because her parents covered for her before, she had learned that there's always a way out of trouble. A confused and angry Katie didn't understand why she had to go to jail. Because her parents were not able to get her out of trouble this time, they were the last people she wanted to see.

So guide your teenager to clean up his messes, clean up his act, and clean up communication. Whether or not your teen's situation is as severe as Katie's or Sam's, give your child the three anchors he or she needs the most.

Clean up your messes. In Sam's case, he has a car to replace, plus legal fees and court costs to pay. If your teen's irresponsible choices lead to legal trouble or damage to someone's property, you'll have to facilitate this repair process, setting up a payment schedule and making sure your teenager stays current on weekly payments until full restitution is made. Avoid the extremes of leaving it up to your teenager to pay the cost or going ahead and paying it yourself.

Clean up your act. Sam needs to connect with a different group of friends. If your teenager has gotten in with the wrong crowd, help him reconnect with friends from a former group—perhaps a sports team or a good church youth group. Or it might mean finding a third group of new friends. You'll have to facilitate this process by opening your home to parties and by showing your teen how to assess and cultivate new friends or reconnect with former friends. (Review chapter 2.)

Clean up communication. If your teenager endangers himself and others, as Sam did, you will need to impose strict rules and limit his freedom. Only honest communication and trustworthy behavior will restore that freedom. Tell your teen he can't go anywhere unless he first lets you know where he's going and with whom. Then when he gets home, he'll have to let you know how things went (see the "Tell me three things" strategy in chapter 1). You'll have to facilitate this process by using good communication skills with your teen (see chapters 1 and 10).

Taking the steps to provide these three anchors will feel like a nightmarish journey for you *and* for your teenager, but it will keep both of you from even nastier nightmares.

CLEAN UP YOUR MESSES

Sam didn't mean to crash the car, but that doesn't change things now that the car is in pieces. His mom doesn't have a car for work, and Sam can't get to after-school activities. Insurance may pay some of the cost of replacing the car; but Sam must pay the rest. He and his parents sat down to talk through the details.

"You'll have to replace the car, Sam."

"I don't have that kind of money!"

"We don't either. We got the car by saving our money and making payments. That's the way you'll replace it."

"But you have a full-time job. I go to school and just work part-time. You have more money than I do."

"If we had crashed the car, we'd be paying the deductible and the cost for a replacement. When you got behind the wheel of the car, you took that responsibility."

"You never told me that! You just said to be careful."

"You've known our family rule for a long time: Whoever breaks it fixes it. I'll admit that we've been too lax, sometimes paying to fix what you broke by accident. But that's not fair to you or to us. You may be making payments for years, but you'll replace the car."

"You are *totally* unfair!"

"Actually this is as fair as we've ever been. Since you crashed it, it's fair for you to replace it."

"But it was an accident!"

"I know you didn't set out to wreck the car, but your choosing to drink made it more likely that you'd have an accident. Even if you'd been totally drug-free you still might have chosen to speed or to be careless or to engage in some other behavior that causes wrecks. Whatever the reason, we still have a car that's totaled. Plus we have court costs and attorney's fees. The results are what count. Good intentions won't replace our car."

Sam and his parents worked out a payment plan. He increased the hours at his part-time job to earn the money more quickly to pay for the damage. That also meant he had less time for running around. Most of his paychecks for several months went into paying for the car. He was allowed to keep about 10 percent to cover gasoline, clothes, music, and going out with friends. Since he was forgoing 90 percent of his pay, he had to order water when he went out with friends, while they enjoyed a burger and fries or pizza and soda pop. Due to diminished funds, he had to postpone buying new CDs and clothes until he paid all that he owed to replace the car.

Sam's parents felt like bullies, and he felt oppressed. But as difficult as this process is, only such a process will lead Sam to become a responsible adult who thinks before going out drinking with friends and who won't endanger his life by drinking and driving. If his parents gave in and covered the legal fees and paid to replace the car, they would build resentment toward Sam, and he would most likely crash another car, having experienced no reason not to do so.

HELP WITH ALCOHOL-RELATED PROBLEMS

Alcohol is the first drug of choice for American teens. Too often parents assume this drug is no big deal. But its problems are long-lasting and frequently fatal. At the very least, teens break the law by drinking alcohol before the legal age. So monitor your teens.

- Know where they are at all times, and let them know that you'll feel free to drive by the house where the party is being held, even to show up at the door. Actually do this at least once to let your teen know you mean business.
- Have parties at your house. As teens have genuine fun at real parties, they'll feel much less inclined to wash their fun away with alcohol.
- If you are the parent of a teen who drinks, Al-Anon will provide you with the support, information, and ideas you need to help your teenager stop. Find a local group in the white pages of your phone book or at www.aa.org.
- If your teenager wants to stop drinking, she or he will find help for doing so at Alateen or Alcoholics Anonymous. Alcoholics Anonymous is a fellowship of men and women working out solutions to their alcoholism. A teenager has to want to go; a parent cannot make him go, nor can a parent go with him. Find a local group in the white pages of your phone book or at www.aa.org.

CLEAN UP YOUR ACT

When Sam first made friends with Drew, he didn't intend to hook up with a party group that left him feeling lonelier than ever. He knows with his head that their raucous laughter is empty laughter. And it became apparent to Sam that when drinking or taking other drugs, no one could make real connections with anyone else. But every kid needs friends, and his emotions tell him these are the only friends he has. When Sam's parents insisted that he cut his ties with Drew and the party crowd, Sam bucked with conviction. He likes these people, he insists, and they like him. His parents see past the bluff.

"Sam, you have had some good times with this bunch, but any group that is bent on drinking will block real fun. You can blame me any time you want, but however you do it, we must find a new group, friends who actually treasure you. You are too important to spend your time with people who don't really care about you. True parties give friends an opportunity to understand and enjoy each other."

Sam's parents helped him invest in new friends who encourage one another and who share life instead of pretending to enjoy it. They opened their home to parties. They spent more on groceries, had to clean the house more often, and lost a lot of sleep. But the joy of hearing *real* conversations between friends who really cared about each other was worth the momentary inconveniences.

Sam started looking around at established groups of friends that didn't depend on alcohol to socialize. He knew a couple of the guys, so at school one day he said, "Hey, if you guys do anything this weekend, I'd love to come along." (See chapter 2 for a sample friend-building process.) As Sam builds new friendships, he'll have an extra hurtle to jump: Many clean-partying kids now think of Sam as a drinker. They may hesitate to invite him for fear he'll bring alcohol or drugs to their gatherings. Or their parents may warn them away from Sam until he proves himself. His parents explain this dynamic to their son, and they help him stay alcohol-free as he rebuilds trust and overcomes a drinking reputation.

CLEAN UP COMMUNICATION

During Sam's partying days, he learned how to hide his plans, his thoughts, and his worries. But his parents know that his success in life depends on his learning to open up about what's going on in his world. If you have a Sam in your family, realize that even the most reticent teenager will talk if given the right parameters. These include:

- Encouragement ("I want to hear about your day, the party, your new friend.")
- Persuasion ("You can't leave the house until you tell me three things about...")

CHOOSE TO PARENT

Parents are called "guardians" for good reasons—we are to guard our teenagers' minds, hearts, bodies, and futures. This is not overprotectiveness; it's responsible parenting. Boundaries both shelter and teach our teenagers. Choose boundaries that give a measure of independence while building trust.

An example: Suppose your daughter is spending time at her boyfriend's house after school when his parents are still at work. Even though both kids are committed Christians, they are setting themselves up for a pregnancy or for the private shame of going too far sexually. Insist that they come to your house (quit your job if you have to) or that they wait to see each other until adults are around. Explain that even the best of us can get into messes without intending to. The solution, for teens and adults both, is to avoid those situations.

- Reward ("Thank you for sharing something that's going on inside. It's not easy to talk about being fearful, insecure, rejected by friends. Your honesty has earned you an extra thirty minutes tonight with your friends.")
- Punishment ("You told us a lie, so you'll have to leave this party and come home with us. Now!")

You as the parent have the hard job of determining when each of the parameters is most appropriate. You must be the prodder, the bad guy, and the checker-upper who gets your teenager back onto the right path. Your son or daughter may choose a wrong action again—he may lie, she may hide things, he may sneak out—and it will be up to you to find out when these things happen and put in place the safety measures necessary to keep it from happening again. When he does something right, it will be just as important that you notice and reward his wise actions and decisions.

Honest communication is hard work (see chapter 1), but without it, your teen will land right back in trouble. So get at least one other adult to hold you accountable to communicate regularly with your teen. You need your mate or a close friend to remind you that all this work really is worth it.

Your teenager won't want your advice, especially at first, but you must give it anyway. Katie's mom, who kept rescuing her shoplifting daughter, had this excuse for not intervening: "Once she told me she didn't want my advice, I stopped giving it to her. If she felt like she could handle it, I didn't want to force my way on her."

This approach makes sense in an adult-to-adult relationship. But your teens are not your peers. Remember that Katie ended up in jail. Your role as a parent is to guide, teach, and instruct, not to leave your sons or daughters with no anchors. Katie drifted into shoplifting not because she wanted to become a criminal, but because she had no parent she knew would listen to her worries and her joys. Her parents were physically there, but they refused to pursue meaningful daily communication. So when Katie became guiltily quiet, they did nothing to find out what was going on in her life. They had not laid a foundation of talking every day, which would have gone a long way in helping Katie resist shoplifting in the first place. Don't let your kids drift. Give them anchors so they can find safe harbors. This does not confine your teenagers, no matter how often they claim otherwise.

Note: Taking your troubled teen to counseling is not a cure-all. It will likely help only if you are part of each session and if you change patterns in your home. Let the goal of counseling be not to "fix" your teen but to grow new patterns of family structure and communication that each family member understands and consistently uses.

SAMPLE BOUNDARIES

Establish firm limits. These boundaries provide the fences that keep kids on the straight and narrow path. Here are a few reasonable expectations:

- Be home by __ o'clock, or you'll lose thirty minutes for every minute you're late.
- Get your chores done before going out, or you'll stay in until the last task is finished.
- Speak kindly to siblings, or lose your computer chat time (or use of the phone) to talk to friends.
- Let me know the starting and ending time of the party, plus the name and phone number of the parents who will supervise, or you don't get to go to that party.
- If you are in by __ o'clock, you can stay out thirty minutes later next weekend.
- Too much restriction? Ponder the way God guides us: He gives us laws to obey until we are ready to act out of heart obedience (see chapter 5).

Don't Teens Have to
Make Mistakes to Learn?

In daily life we learn from some mistakes. Isn't the same true for teenagers? Not when you consider that many mistakes could easily kill him.

When a teenager makes a mistake over what to wear to a party, it can lead to momentary embarrassment. You can say, "You've learned the wisdom of calling first to check on what other kids are planning to wear." But accidentally killing a person with a car after taking a couple of drinks isn't a mistake you can follow with, "Now you've learned your lesson. Go on with life." The victims of a car crash can't rise from the grave to continue on with life. Mistakes like these cause permanent damage.

We don't feed steak to infants simply because they'll have teeth in a year or two. We don't let twelve-year-olds drive the family on vacation simply because they'll get a permit in three years or so. So why do we fall for the myth "He'll be on his own soon, so I might as well let him start making mistakes now." This myth has been so frequently repeated that many parents accept it as fact. Mistakes now don't mean fewer mistakes later. Mistakes now mean your teen doesn't have the wisdom to make wise choices, and he could ruin the rest of his life with one lapse of judgment.

So loan your wisdom to your teen, even when he's in college, until he can practice that wisdom for himself.

Nowhere in the Bible does God urge mistake making as a learning method. The word "mistake" doesn't even occur in the *King James* translation of the Bible, and it occurs only five times in the *New International Version*. None of these references speak about learning from mistakes. Fixing mistakes, yes. Regretting mistakes, definitely. But

MISTAKES THAT DAMAGE YOUR TEEN

- A single episode of wild driving can lead to life in a wheel-chair. So let your teen know she'll pay any speeding tickets, traffic violations, and the insurance hikes that result. Calculate how much money that could actually be and discuss it with your teen.

- A series of no-homework nights can lead to failing a course, which reduces the chance of obtaining scholarships and being accepted into a good college. It could prevent living in the honors dorm at college, which means living on a floor with the party crowd, which means not getting as much from college and not getting into grad-uate school. So insist that your teen do his homework every night, letting him watch television or have free time only after it's fin-ished. Check and quiz as needed to verify studying.

- A single sexual liaison can lead to a lifetime of poverty while par-enting a child born too soon. It can also pass on an STD that might lead to infertility, cancer, and even death. So insist that your teen not go to a date's house without an adult around. And guide your teen and his or her date to plan their evenings so they have more to do than park on a lonely road. Assure them that at any time you might check to see if they are where they said they'd be. If your teen does get pregnant, encourage adoption so the baby can have two parents. If your daughter or son presses for abortion, help them avoid multiplying their sin. Put them in touch with a cri-sis pregnancy counselor.

- A single drunk-driving experience can lead to injury, death, or a jail sentence. So take the car away for any incidences of alcohol use or wild driving. Return it only after a time period that matches the severity of the offense.

mistakes are not championed as a learning approach. Instead the Bible stresses parents' responsibility to deliberately show their children what to do and how to do it.

Somebody has to be the adult, and it's you, the parent. The choice to "let them make their own mistakes" is an excuse some parents use to avoid doing the hard stuff. They don't want to bother walking alongside their teens to correct missteps and prod them back onto the right path. They'd rather just pray about it and leave the outcome to God. But God has already answered that prayer by showing us what our responsibility is as parents. Parents are to guide their kids in the right path (see Deuteronomy 6:1-3,6-7; Proverbs 22:6).

Without active guidance from parents, our teens can't find the way they should go. Parents who abdicate the God-given responsibility to raise their teenagers end up producing teens who cause tremendous pain for others. These teens break their own hearts, they break the hearts of their parents, and they break the hearts of their children and grandchildren by setting into motion destructive family patterns that can be nearly impossible to break (see Exodus 20:5-6).

So reject the "let them make their own mistakes" myth and instead proactively teach your teen. Show him how to get back onto the right path of healthy friendships and fun making. Show him why Christians really should have more fun. Show him how to have parties that make kids want to come back. Show him how to have a genuine heart-to-heart conversation with someone who matters to him. Walk alongside him at every juncture. One step will lead to another until the steps mark a wise path to follow in life. As your teenager walks steadily in the path of parties without alcohol, picking friends who enjoy each other rather than try to impress each other, and truthfully letting his parents know what he does, he'll create a smooth road of genuine life sharing and enjoyable conversation. Because this road is a pleasant one, he won't easily veer from it. He'll choose a spouse from the group of responsible, level-headed kids, and their children will enjoy the blessing of their parents' wise choices and habits.

Your job is not to make your teenager happy; it's to raise a teenager who becomes a whole individual. But, delightfully, as teenagers learn to make good choices, they find happiness. So do their children and their children's children. And the good continues to bless future generations.

ACTION STEPS

No matter how severe your teen's behavior, find a path that pulls him away from the wrong and back to the right. Find this sure path by searching the Scriptures, through consulting wise advisors, and by noticing the way God teaches you. Then walk your teenager through that same path until he stops the dangerous behavior and starts a good behavior in its place. Don't take the easy road of doing nothing.

What Scripture says: "Hear, O Israel, and be careful to obey so that it may go well with you and that you may increase greatly.... These commandments that I give you today are to be upon your hearts. Impress them on your children. Talk about them when you sit at home and when you walk along the road, when you lie down and when you get up" (Deuteronomy 6:3,6-7).

Explain to your teen: "I love you too much to let you destroy yourself with this. We are family, and we will choose not just to talk about the right thing but to do it."

7

MY TEENAGER AVOIDS CHURCH

STAND YOUR GROUND. SHE WON'T
BECOME A PRODIGAL!

"Can I *please* stay home from church this morning?" Shelley begged.

Shelley's parents had noticed a loss of enthusiasm toward youth group meetings, but they hadn't realized things were this serious. "Why do you want to stay home, Shelley?"

"Church is boring, and I can worship God better in my own backyard."

"That may be, but there are still good reasons for going to church every week."

"Can't I skip just this once, Dad? Please?"

"Have you and God had a falling out, Shelley?"

"No, God and I are fine. It's church I don't like."

The reason teens avoid church is seldom problems with God. It's usually friend troubles, loneliness, real or imagined shame, or a disinterested church youth worker. But because church helps the God connection happen, we must equip our teens to move past the barriers and create a healthy church experience. Teens need regular connections with God *and* regular connections with people who love God to help them master whatever struggles and triumphs they experience in daily life. Church is not the only place these connections can occur, of course, but it is a foundational place. So make church a nonnegotiable in your family.

Think School

Your teenager's problem with church may not be that big of a deal. She may simply be tired and not want to get up early—not very different from what happens on a normal school day. Your teen has likely begged you to let her stay home from school "just this once." Perhaps she was up late the night before doing homework. But you insisted that she go to school without fretting that she would hate education for the rest of her life. You assumed she would find a way to learn and to cope with her fatigue. And you supplied the regular guidance and encouragement that helped her get to class week after week throughout the school year.

This same action is the first line of defense for solving the I-don't-want-to-go-to-church problem. Going to school is essential for a good education. Going to church is essential for forming and maintaining good spiritual connections. So get your teen there every Sunday.

All the logic in the world won't convince your teenager that she needs to be at church when she's snuggled in a warm, cozy bed. But decisive action will. Just like you do on the days she doesn't want to go to school, get her up and get her to church. For Shelley it went like this:

"Shelley, you're right that church is sometimes boring. You're right that you can worship God in the backyard. You're right that you and God are doing fine. But the fact remains that you need connections at church, and the church needs you. Church attendance is a non-negotiable in our family, just like school. So roll out and let's get going. Whatever condition you're in at 8:45 is the condition you'll be in when you get in the car with us to leave. You can finish getting ready in the car if it comes to that, but you'll be in the car at 8:45."

"But that's only forty minutes from now!"

"You'd best get moving then!"

WHY TEENS BUCK SPIRITUALITY

Teenagers crave a relationship with the God who is bigger than they are. But some life experiences push them away from God.

- Maybe someone erroneously attributed to God something he didn't do—such as the death of a beloved friend of your teen.
- Maybe other teens at church are unkind or aloof. Because those same kids have charmed the youth group leaders, the leaders regard them as being the truly spiritual kids. Your teen sees otherwise.
- Maybe your teen has asked questions at church about God's existence and why things are the way they are but her questions have been wrongly trivialized or squashed.
- Maybe you, as parents, have talked about God but then acted in ways that contradict your stated beliefs. Your teen sees no reason to maintain a personal loyalty to God since you don't demonstrate it.
- Maybe she's tired of seeing bickering and power plays at church and wants to see genuine Christian love instead.
- Maybe you, as a parent, spend all your time with people at church. You have no time to listen to your teen's stories, questions, and concerns. She rejects church because it pulls you away from her.

What to do? Help your teenager explore God's real character rather than believe the inaccurate representations. Agree with your teen that unkindness and immorality contradict true Christianity. Encourage her to freely ask you questions about God so she will be solidly based on truth and not feeling. Serve God consistently in your own life, and weekly reserve time in your schedule for your teen.

Parents often feel like ogres for making their teenagers go to church, especially if things have been unhappy there. Will missing only one Sunday really make a difference? Absolutely.

In theory it makes sense to give your teens a break. *After a week away,* you reason, *she'll feel refreshed and ready to come back to church next Sunday.* You've experienced that same refreshment after a week away from work. But with church, just the opposite happens. When your teen misses even one Sunday, she'll feel like a visitor when she returns. The happenings of the week, or weeks, when she was absent create a foundation of inside jokes and remember-whens that your teen won't be a part of. She'll feel even more alienated than before.

If you let your teens skip church, they won't come back. So insist on weekly Sunday morning attendance and at least one other church activity during the week, such as a midweek Bible study or youth group meeting. Unlike taking a vacation from work, the refreshment comes from being at church, not from staying away.

The second line of defense is this: As you insist on church attendance, do everything you can to make it a positive experience. Show your teens how to "do church." Help your teenagers discover why the people at church really do need them. Suggest ways to connect with their peers as well as how to serve another group, perhaps by volunteering to usher or prepare bulletins or other worship-service items once a month or regularly visiting older members to do yard work or other needed chores. Help her work around the ornery people at your church—and they're in *every* church. These four actions can help your teen build healthy church involvement:

- You gotta go, no matter how you feel.
- You gotta find a solution, no matter what the struggle.
- You gotta give more than you take.
- You gotta honor God on more than just Sunday mornings.

Go No Matter How You Feel

Whether they've grown up in church or are new to it, every teenager goes through a time of not wanting to attend church. In my twenty-eight years of youth work, I've only met two teens who didn't fight this battle. The Bible makes it clear that adults fight this problem too, as evidenced by the exhortation of Hebrews 10:24-25 to not neglect the opportunity to meet with other believers. So start by recognizing church involvement as a universal struggle, but one that needs deliberate attention.

Ask your teen, "What makes you not want to go?" and then really listen. When you understand the problems, you can give your teen the best strategies for managing them. Arrange to have this listening time *after* church, not while you're struggling to get your teen ready to leave on Sunday morning.

What makes teenagers avoid church? She may say she's not comfortable at church. He may say no one likes him there. She may say that no one would miss her if she were absent. He may say it's boring. She may say no one wants to listen to what she asks or thinks. He may say there's too much cruelty in the church.

Your teen may be exactly right. The tricky part is that the solution to these problems is to establish and maintain relationships at church, not to boycott it. We work through our struggles only through shared experiences with other Christians and through intentional service. Teenagers and youth workers must practice interaction for real fellowship and service to take root. Pray for and cherish good youth leaders who can nurture your teen once you get her to church. Consider becoming one of those workers yourself. Then show the teens at your church how to interact and serve.

Shelley's parents, after a week-in-week-out struggle, have been getting her to church on time. But after a few weeks they have discovered she has been hiding in the rest room rather than going to the high school class. She and several girlfriends excuse themselves to go to the rest room and never come back. Shelley's parents have asked the teacher not to let her leave the class, but the teacher hasn't stopped it.

They must act on this pattern of skipping Sunday school class. It's not the teacher's responsibility to keep them there. Parents are the only ones responsible for getting their teenagers to show up and actually

---

ADVICE WITH SKIN ON IT

Just reading the principles in this book won't be enough. You need real live people to show you how to teach your teen to honor Jesus daily. Possibilities include:

Your spouse. You and your spouse know your kids the best and love them the most. So talk things over to prove that two heads are truly better than one. What Mom doesn't think of, Dad will, and what doesn't occur to Dad, Mom can suggest.

Other parents of teenagers. Don't share war stories with other parents. Your teens need to know that what they tell you is held in confidence. But garner wisdom from other parents with neutral questions like, "How do you encourage your three to enjoy church so much?" or "What rules does your family use to enforce a curfew?"

Wise members of your extended family. Grandparents have the perspective of parenting children from birth to independence. They won't be right about everything, but their perspective can keep you from tunnel vision. Then you won't panic too much or ignore too much.

The Bible. The foundation for all of the above is God's Word. Begin a list of Bible verses that demonstrate the character you want your teen to express. Then work toward teaching those character traits. Samples: Galatians 5:22-23, Philippians 2:4, and Titus 3:8.

---

participate in the activities at church. The class you're teaching, or any other conflicting church responsibility that you have, takes a backseat to your teen's spiritual connections. If she hides in the bathroom, physically accompany her to the classroom and park yourself outside until the class is over. Be subtle about it, but put yourself where you will notice if she leaves. If there are two doors to the classroom, station your spouse at the other door. If there are three doors, enlist a confidential friend.

For Shelley, it went something like this:

"Shelley, starting this Sunday you have to not only go to church, but you also have to go to class."

"I do, Dad!"

"You may go *into* class, but you haven't been staying there. You and some others have been gathering in the bathroom."

"Sometimes ya gotta go, Dad."

"It doesn't take forty-five minutes."

"Have you been spying on me?"

"Yes, I have."

"That doesn't show much trust!"

"Trust is earned by good behavior; it's not something you use as an excuse to get away with wrong behavior."

"But parents are supposed to trust their kids."

"We trust you whenever we see evidence of trustworthy behavior."

"I'll act trustworthy. I promise!"

"Yes, you will. I'll help you keep your promise."

"What do you mean?"

"I'll follow you, Secret Service–style, to Bible study. Then I'll sit in a place where you can't see me but I can see if you leave the classroom."

"That's totally unfair!"

"Actually, it's quite fair. If I ask something of you, it's my job to make certain you do it."

"I could go out the back door you know."

"Mom will be at that door."

"You're kidding!"

"Nope."

"But, Dad, what about the class you teach? I'd hate for you to miss that!"

"You're very thoughtful, Shelley, but you come first. I have a sub."

"But, Dad!"

"No ifs, ands, or buts. You'll stay in class, and I'll make certain of it."

"What if I really *do* have to go to the bathroom?"

"You can go before class and then hold it until class is over."

"Dad!"

"That's the way it will be."

On the way home the following Sunday, after Shelley stayed in class, her parents asked how things went. "What was a good thing that happened in Bible study today? Did you meet anyone new or reach out to anyone who was struggling? What did you think of the pastor's sermon?"

Shelley answered with "I don't know" and "Not much."

Her parents wondered if they'd done the right thing. But after a few weeks she began talking about the events of the morning. These conversations helped her parents help Shelley do church well. They could highlight her good insights ("It made sense to me that gossip is as destructive as murder because…") as well as help her know how to gracefully disagree ("I thought what they said about fellowship was a little far-fetched…"). It also helped them bless her good actions ("I've been sitting by Cecelia, and she talks more now"). They also walked with her through the agonies ("Yes, you're right that he shouldn't have done that"). If your own teenager stays quiet after several weeks of your asking questions about his or her church experience, try the communication principles from chapter 1.

FIND A SOLUTION TO
WHATEVER STRUGGLES COME

As Shelley's dad listened to her on several drives home from church, he discovered that his daughter's struggles centered around feeling insignificant:

"So you feel like nobody at church likes you?" he asked, after she complained of a lack of connection with the other kids.

"That's right."

"What has happened to make you feel that way?"

"The teacher acts like Todd is some sort of Bible scholar, but he never gives me credit for anything I try to contribute."

"Bummer."

"And the entire class adores Todd. They think he's more spiritual than the rest of us."

"Ouch."

"I've seen how snobby he is at school. The Bible study teacher and the other kids don't know because they don't go to our school."

"We all have our secret sins, don't we?"

"Yep. But his sins are no secret to anyone who attends our school."

People at church sometimes have blind spots that impact your teenager negatively. Shelley's teacher has chosen to favor a student who parrots all the correct answers. This student may not live everything he says in class, but the teacher ignores this because Todd makes the teacher feel smart. Singling out certain students for special treatment is a significant problem in too many churches. It usually happens accidentally, but being unaware of it makes it no less destructive. It makes Shelley not want to have anything to do with church and its favoritism games. Staying home won't solve the problem. Instead, she and her parents need to work together to find a solution:

"Shelley, your teacher likely favors Todd because his answers make him feel like a great teacher. But the Bible says each Christian has critical gifts and ideas to contribute to the body of Jesus Christ. No one should be elevated above the others."

"My teacher certainly doesn't believe that."

"Probably not, at least not in practice. Some teachers are better than others at recognizing the value of each student. Most don't even realize they're showing favoritism, something clearly forbidden in the Bible [see James 2:1-9]. They're just nervous about teaching, so they let a particular student make them feel better. Maybe you could affirm other students' answers to start the process of valuing everybody."

"Nobody listens to me."

"Maybe not everybody, but I guarantee you that somebody does."

"I doubt it."

"I don't. I've seen the gift of encouragement that you have."

"What do you mean?"

"When you say kind and true things to people, they believe you. They feel empowered to keep doing the right thing."

"All I do is talk."

"But you use your words the way Jesus would. That's very impressive."

"Thanks."

"Hang in there with this teacher, and next year things may get a bit better."

"Can I tell him you think he plays favorites?"

"I don't think that would be a good idea. Let's just keep this between the two of us."

"How 'bout I'll keep it secret if you'll let me skip Bible study."

"Sorry."

Shelley's dad felt like marching over to the church and demanding that this teacher be replaced. But he also knew that the church has many strengths that overcome this teacher's foibles, such as the pastor's overall stance of valuing every youth, weekly encouragement e-mails from the youth minister, and monthly opportunities for teenagers to participate in mission projects. So he helped Shelley recognize and value those strengths. He also volunteered to substitute in Shelley's class.

For a teenager to learn to do church well takes time, persistence, and action on the part of her parents. That starts with getting out of bed on Sunday mornings and going to church. For Shelley, getting there didn't guarantee smooth sailing. Her teacher was a shipmaster with inadequate skills. But Shelley would miss the whole trip if she didn't get into the boat. Her parents started working to equip her to manage the waves and notice the sunshine. She began to focus on other youth leaders who valued every teenager. She grew spiritually through what the pastor was teaching. And she used her gift of encouragement to help other believers. While sailing at church Shelley and other believing teens formed bonds, wrestled with important spiritual truths, and explored ways to live for God during the other six days of the week.

GIVE MORE THAN YOU TAKE

Once your teen is at church and working through any problems, help her see church as part of her bigger purpose in life. Church is not a place to go and get, but a group to join and serve. If you or your teen attends church expecting only to receive, you will both grow cranky, critical, and unsatisfied. But when you and your teen believe you are significant parts of the church's ministry to others, you will find ways to give even when things get crazy. Your church will delight in your teen's participation.

Every Christian matters critically to the health of the entire church (see Romans 12:4-8; 1 Corinthians 12:12-27; Ephesians 4:11-13). Your teenager's involvement is critical to your local church body. If your teen doesn't participate, the church will miss her unique spiritual gifts. Because you see your teen daily, you are the best one to discern his or her gifts. Also the home is the center of spiritual training (see Deuteronomy 6:6-7). So every week find new ways to affirm the spiritual gift you see in your teenager, and help your teen use this gift. To identify and prompt your teenager's gifts, think about her strengths and abilities.

THE GIFT OF PROPHECY

Your teenager may have the spiritual gift of prophesy (see Romans 12:6; 1 Corinthians 12:10,28) if she asks lots of hard questions, grows impatient with churchy talk that seems to lack sincerity, or sometimes irritates people with her wise ideas (recall how few people appreciated prophets in the Bible). Questions to prompt your teen's expression of the gift of prophesy include:

- How could you ask your questions in ways that get people thinking rather than make them want to argue with you?
- How can you time your comments so they motivate positive change?
- How can you affirm people when they ask hard questions, assuring them that asking questions leads to finding the answer?

THE GIFT OF SERVING

Your teenager may have the spiritual gift of serving (see Romans 12:7) if he does what needs doing without being asked, if he doesn't seek credit for what he does, or if he can motivate others to work together to accomplish tasks. Questions to prompt your teen's expression of this gift include:

- What secret act of service might you do to solve a problem no one has yet solved?
- What would make that hard project more fun (singing as you do it, teaming up with someone else)?
- What words or actions show appreciation to people who help get the project done (so they will want to serve more often)?

THE GIFT OF TEACHING

Your teenager may have the spiritual gift of teaching (see Romans 12:7; 1 Corinthians 12:28) if she finds new ways to describe classic truths, if her eyes light up when someone "gets it," or if she wants to volunteer to help younger children in Sunday school. Questions to prompt your teen's expression of the gift of teaching include:

- What item or picture would Jesus use to make that truth even clearer?
- Could students create an object to take home with them to remind them of God's love?
- What would help you see, hear, taste, smell, or touch that truth? How might you use that approach in teaching the Bible?

THE GIFT OF ENCOURAGEMENT

Your teenager may have the spiritual gift of encouragement (see Romans 12:8) if being around people energizes him, if he speaks words that keep people going, or if his heart breaks when someone else hurts. Questions to prompt your teen's expression of this gift include:

- What actions would show God's love without using words?
- What words would help in this situation?
- What do you like people to say or do when you have been through a situation similar to your friend's? (The experience could be a happy or sad one.) How will you do the same?

THE GIFT OF HELPS

Your teenager may have the spiritual gift of helps—which involves contributing to the needs of others (see 1 Corinthians 12:28)—if she finds creative ways to help people do what needs to get done, if she has extraordinary sensitivity to what individuals go through, and if she helps without being asked. Questions to prompt your teen's expression of the gift of helps include:

- What personal needs can be identified behind that action or feeling?
- How would Jesus meet that person's need or motivate the person to help himself?
- How could you imitate Jesus in helping that person?

THE GIFT OF GIVING

Your teenager may have the spiritual gift of giving (see Romans 12:8) if he gives things away without worrying about whether he'll want them again, if he finds ways to make a small amount of something multiply, or if he listens fervently and loses track of time. Questions to prompt your teen's expression of this gift include:

- What kind of attention would make that person happy?
- What resources do you have, or have access to, that could meet that need?
- What generous actions bring out the best in people?

THE GIFT OF ADMINISTRATION

Your teenager may have the spiritual gift of administration (see 1 Corinthians 12:28) if she's able to get the whole group doing what it needs to do without their realizing she's "bossing" them, or if she can get people to understand why they need to do something. Questions to prompt your teen's expression of administration include:

- What instructions or information does this group need to do its job with happiness and effectiveness?
- How can we break that big project down into workable steps?
- What are the specific steps that will help achieve our desired goal?

THE GIFT OF EVANGELISM

Your teenager may have the spiritual gift of evangelism (see Ephesians 4:11) if he wants more than anything else for each person to be saved, if his heart breaks when someone rejects Jesus, or if he thinks of new ways to help people understand the gospel. Questions to prompt your teen's expression of this gift include:

- What evidence do you see that she is hungry for Jesus?
- How might you tap into that hunger and show how Jesus meets that need?
- What words or illustrations would invite that person to Jesus?

THE GIFT OF LEADERSHIP

Your teenager may have the spiritual gift of leadership (see Romans 12:8) if she doesn't mind doing the same things she asks other people to do, if she motivates without even realizing it, if other people imitate what she does. (Hint: Bossing and talking are seldom indicators of biblical leadership.) Questions to prompt your teen's expression of the gift of leadership include:

- Who do you like to follow or imitate?
- What actions and attitudes does that person express?
- How will you lead with those good actions rather than by bossing or telling?

THE GIFT OF MERCY

Your teenager may have the spiritual gift of mercy (see Romans 12:8) if he is quick to forgive, if he readily understands why someone may have chosen to do the wrong thing, or if he feels the joy and sadness that people around him feel. Questions to prompt your teen's expression of mercy include:

- What actions will show tenderness to the people you see today?
- How can you give someone else a fresh start—this is the goal of mercy, to turn from wrong and begin to do right.
- Who needs a special expression of Jesus' love today?

No matter what your teen's spiritual gift, help her express it with her peers as well as with others in the church. Just don't let her "hide" in the nursery or through volunteering with another age group every week. She must minister to others and be ministered to in regular connection with fellow teenagers, or she will continue to feel like a fifth wheel.

SHOULD YOU SWITCH CHURCHES?

Most of a teenager's church problems can be addressed with consistent attendance and practice in people-relating skills. You, as parents, can guide both of those processes. But sometimes the problem really does lie with the church. To help determine if your current church is the right place for your family, get to the bottom-line issues: Does this church honor Jesus in its youth program and in its overall ministry? Are all members of your family able to participate well and in healthy ways? If you answered no to either of those questions, it might be time to look into another church. Before deciding, however, consider these factors:

AN UNHEALTHY YOUTH CULTURE

A church's youth culture can become unhealthy, even cruel. Perhaps the group is mostly intellectuals and the kids snub anyone who struggles in school. Perhaps the group goes to clubs on the weekend, sneaking in those who are underage. Maybe the group inadvertently vandalizes construction sites with a "fellowship" game that includes throwing small bags of flour at each other. Most times such cultures develop by accident, but the results are still devastating.

LEADERS WHO SHOW FAVORITISM

Too many church youth leaders categorize the kids in two groups: the "leaders" or the "spiritual" kids versus the "followers"—those who "need to grow." This approach flies in the face of the Bible's teaching that the church is the body of Christ, where no Christian is more or less important than another. It also encourages faking it to become part of the spiritual in-group. A healthy church values the contributions of every member as critical to the whole.

DISCOMFORT WITH HONEST QUESTIONS

Some youth leaders discourage kids by stifling their honest questions. They try to make teens believe that "doubts are bad" and "we just have to trust God enough to not question." Such a view actually keeps kids from growing. Spiritual growth can only happen when teens are permitted to ask and wrestle with the hard questions of life.

Lack of Deliberate Spiritual Training

Teenagers, like adults, need help in practically living for Jesus. Nobody is born knowing how to honor Jesus through friendships, schoolwork, and church. Parents and church leaders must teach teenagers how to live in obedience to Scripture through both advice and modeling. They must continue to grow themselves. Find a church that intentionally shows teens and all members how to do the right thing in all areas of life.

Inadequate Boundaries

When a youth group assembles, teenagers will take risks and act dangerously unless adult leaders enforce consistent boundaries. Youth group members will hurt one another through cruel pranks, they will congregate in the parking lot rather than come into Bible study, or they will sneak out at night during youth trips. Too often these behaviors are applauded or even initiated by adult leaders trying to be "cool." Choose a church with leaders who are secure adults and who will consistently enforce rules that help everyone become his very best. Sample rules: no people slamming; treasure what everyone says in Bible study; leave the campground nicer than you found it; play only music with lyrics that honor God.

Conflict Among Leaders

It's difficult for teenagers to get along when staff ministers don't get along. Everyone has differences of opinion, but when tension prevails, it will filter into every ministry. Choose instead a church with a cooperative pastoral staff, staff members who enjoy and encourage each other both publicly and privately. That togetherness and body-of-Christ approach will filter down to the youth.

If you feel that your church fails consistently in any of these areas, prayerfully consider seeking a church with a healthy spiritual atmosphere. If you do decide to switch, make sure you do so as a family rather than send your teen to another church.

SPILL SPIRITUALITY OVER INTO LIFE

What our teens experience at church means little if they don't live it outside the church walls. So as your teens form relationships and find purpose at church, let that spill over into daily living. Each activity of every day is an opportunity for spiritual expression. The way your teen talks to siblings, the way she uses the telephone, the way he finishes homework—all of these actions either honor or dishonor God. The other chapters in this book detail nine ways to honor God besides involvement at church. Those include using good conversation skills, relating honorably to friends, turning from mistakes, displaying good work habits, choosing right behavior, stopping sin patterns, earning and managing money, managing emotions, and living by rules and within set boundaries. Parents are the key players in helping teens establish these wise spiritual habits.

Jesus explained that healthy spirituality must be taught (see Matthew 28:20). Becoming a believer is the first step. Then it's up to us as parents to teach our teens to obey everything that Jesus has commanded. He will be with us to show us how, but we've got to go ahead and do what he shows us. And we must find a church that helps us in that process.

Whether in the church building or outside of it, cultivate a what-would-Jesus-do stance to form a foundation for contented living. Suppose your daughter has been locked in the bathroom for over an hour, primping and changing her clothes one more time. She has promised her brother she'd fly a kite with him before she goes to tonight's party, but she hasn't yet done that. He's been waiting since Monday because she had so much homework to do all week.

THE SPIRITUALITY GAME

Spirituality is not carrying a big Bible and going to church all the time. It's letting God guide each action of the day. Play a game with your teens in which they challenge you to name a way to be spiritual in a certain circumstance. Then you get to ask them.

Samples:

How can I be spiritual in playing cards? *Say, "Anybody can make a mistake" when your partner plays the wrong card, rather than, "You dummy! You caused us to lose!"*

How can I be spiritual while reading? *You pick magazines and books that give real answers rather than urge you to buy a certain makeup so guys will notice you.*

How can I be spiritual when washing dishes? *You invite someone to keep you company so you can build a relationship while working. Or when you're alone, you work just as hard to do the task excellently so it honors God (see Colossians 3:23).*

How can I be spiritual while studying math? *You thank God for ordering the universe. Then ask him to help you use that order to understand math.*

How do I show spirituality while talking to my sister? *You listen with rapt attention so you can rejoice with her when she's happy and cry with her when she's sad (see Romans 12:15).*

How do I show spirituality while eating dinner? *You practice hospitality by making every person at the table feel a part of things (see Romans 12:13).*

"Must be a girl thing," you conclude as your daughter remains locked in the bathroom. "Guys wouldn't worry so much about their looks." But guy or girl, the issue is the same: Your daughter is more interested in the party than the commitment she made to spend time with her brother. And she might be so anxious about the party that she is focusing too much on her looks and not enough on having fun.

So you initiate some spiritual instruction.

"Honey, your brother has been patiently waiting since Monday for you two to fly his kite."

"But, Dad, one more day won't make that much difference."

"Not to you maybe. But to him another day is huge. Keeping your word is an important way to honor God."

"God won't mind. It's not like it's a Bible study or anything."

"This may actually be more important than a Bible study. It's the acting out of what you learned when studying the Scripture—offering yourself as a living sacrifice, to be used by God. Your spending time with Carlos shows him that God can be trusted and that God cares about him."

"But I'm not God!"

"You're his representative. God uses people to love other people."

"Well, I love Carlos. You know that and he knows that, but this party is really important to me."

"Yes it is, and we'll make a way for you to get there. There is plenty of time to look good, party hearty, and love your brother all in the same day. So I'll give you ten more minutes. Then you can go kite flying. If you don't spend a full hour with your brother, though, you'll forgo the party altogether."

"That's not fair! I can't get ready in ten more minutes! And flying a kite will mess up my hair!"

"It's very fair. You knew about the kite flying. You knew about the party. I'll help you not worry so much about your appearance that you miss the real reason for parties—to enjoy the people who are there. People really do care more about how you treat them than about how you look."

"What about thirty minutes of kite flying."

"Nope. A full hour. And I'll be listening. For every time you act impatiently toward your brother, you'll lose thirty minutes of party time."

"But you know how much I've been looking forward to this party!"

"Then I'd wait to finish doing your hair until after the kite flying. And stop worrying so much about your appearance that you can't relax enough to enjoy the party."

By using active parenting, you give your daughter the boundary of spiritual responsibility—find time to look good, follow through on your commitment to your brother, and have a great time at the party, all to God's honor. We have to impose this responsibility on our teens until they are mature enough to impose it on themselves, just like God does for us (see Psalm 32:8-9). As your daughter follows through on God-honoring behaviors, she has opportunities to fulfill God's purposes for her.

Guide your teen to find God's purposes day in and day out. How should I spend this hour? What does God want me to think about while I'm driving to a friend's house? How will I mow the lawn to God's glory? In so doing, you and your teen will find delight in a life lived to God's honor and shared with God's people. And you will learn right back from your teen just how to honor God with the minutes of your own day.

ACTION STEPS

Because we need one another to live out our faith well, equip your son or daughter to connect regularly with other Christian teenagers. An honorable church is the most likely place for this to happen.

What Scripture says: "Two are better than one.... [H]ow can one keep warm alone?" (Ecclesiastes 4:9,11).

Explain to your teen: "Not all Christians are nice, but truly nice people have God as their foundation. To help us make connections with people who truly honor God, we'll be involved in church every week. At church, we will serve others and receive from others. By doing both we'll practice a good and healthy faith."

8

MY TEENAGER DOESN'T WANT

TO WORK

WHO DOES? YOU CAN SHOW HIM HOW

Sixteen-year-old Robert just doesn't get it. He empties the gas tank and forgets to fill it up. He orders both a soft drink and dessert every time he eats out. And he won't even consider going to cheaper restaurants. His parents give him an allowance so he can learn to manage his finances, but so far it doesn't seem to be working.

Robert has the use of a cell phone but is expected to limit his monthly use to a certain number of minutes. He also has free access to the family car. But Robert goes over on his cell-phone minutes and incurs extra charges. He asks for advances on his allowance, and he forgets to change the oil in the car. When will he learn to manage money and to control the things that cost money?

He'll begin to learn when he has to fund his own expenses.

Very few teenagers jump at the chance to go to work. But all teenagers want money to spend. Money is the ticket to getting the things they want and to going where they want to go. So to motivate a good work ethic, tie the responsibility of working to available cash and to freedom.

Stop funding key areas so your teenager can learn to manage them on his own. The three best areas to delegate to teens are clothing, transportation, and spending money. You might delegate one at a time or several at once. Here's how Robert's mom presented things to him:

"Robert, it won't be long before you'll be living on your own. To keep from having to take on all the responsibilities of life at once, we want you to take on just a few at a time. Beginning this Friday, your dad and I will no longer provide your spending money or pay for your gasoline or clothes. You'll need to get a job to cover these expenses. You can continue to use my car if we work out ahead of time who needs it when. But you'll have to put gasoline in it every time you drive."

"But I don't have time to work! You know how crazy my schedule is already."

"I'll be glad to help you rearrange it. I remember that feeling myself—where will I find more hours to earn money? But it's time to take this step toward adulthood."

"That's okay. I'm perfectly happy for you to pay the bills."

"So are most people! We'd all love to have someone else pay the way for us. I can't change that, but I can help you. As long as I continue to pay your bills, you'll remain dependent. I want you to be able to make your own wise choices. Managing money is the first major step toward that goal."

"I have enough money for now, and my clothes are fine. Plus I have money in the bank that I can pull out for spending money. So can I hold off on getting a job until next year?"

"Nope. That bank account is for college, so we'll block withdrawals on that for now. If you want spending money so you can run around with your friends, you'll need to have a job by the end of next week."

"What if no one's hiring?"

"Then you can spend that weekend finding someone who is. The job you find may not be your first choice, but you can always work in a grocery store or fast-food place until you get something more to your liking."

"But I don't even know how to start! Do I just march in and say, 'Give me a job'?"

"I'll show you the steps to take. Here, I'll write them down for you."

NINE GOOD JOBS

"There's no place to work in this town!" most teens claim. So sit down with your teenager to brainstorm possibilities, explaining that sometimes he must accept his second or third choice before moving up to his first:

- Fast-food restaurants: Choose to be a cook, cashier, order assembler.
- Fine restaurants: You can be a greeter, waitress, cook, or busboy.
- Retail: You might wait on customers, restock shelves, or work the cash register.
- Hardware stores: Like to fix and build things? Join a team that helps people who enjoy doing the same thing.
- Construction: If your teen wants to build muscle and doesn't mind a little dirt, this job can teach teamwork.
- Office helper: If your teen wants to be a lawyer, suggest she type and file at a lawyer's office (or veterinary clinic or school or whatever matches your teen's interest). Even sweeping floors at these businesses can give your teen a feel for the work.
- Janitorial services: Cleaning well can earn big bucks and can often be done on a flexible schedule.
- Factory work: Everything from filling orders to assembling automobiles provides opportunities to see the end result of hard work.
- Agricultural work: Join seasonal teams that bale hay, harvest vegetables, or perform other farm labor.

Show Him the Steps

Robert was not thrilled about getting a job. But knowing that a job would bring him far more benefits than pain, his parents worked out a plan. They gave him two weeks to land a job. To make that goal achievable, they built in intermediate deadlines, such as the day to bring home job applications, the day to turn the applications back in, and the number of places he should schedule interviews. They also talked about what to say when applying for a job, how many hours to ask for, and more. For a teenager who has never held down a job, it's helpful to practice useful questions, such as:

- "I'd like to apply for a part-time job. May I pick up an application?"
- "I'd like to work ten to fifteen hours a week. Who can I talk to about this?"
- "I'm a hard worker and I'd like to work here. How do I apply?"

To begin the process and keep it moving forward, Robert's mom gave him a list of steps. The first would take place the following Friday afternoon. Here are the steps she included in the list:

- Day One (Friday): Pick up an application and bring it home so we can practice filling out applications and preparing for interviews. Then achieve the goal of filling out six job applications within the first week.
- Day Nine (the following Saturday): By this day finish filling out all the applications and return them to the places of business. (Some will get filled out on the spot and left with the store manager during the initial visit.)
- Day Twelve (the following Tuesday): By this day call each prospective employer back, explain that you turned in an application a few days earlier, and ask when you could come for an interview.

- Day Thirteen (Wednesday): By this day list questions to ask and answer during the upcoming interview(s). Select appropriate clothing to wear.
- The days following: Show up on time for all interviews. Report for follow-up interviews if needed. If you receive a job offer, don't make a final decision immediately. First discuss it with parents.

Robert and his mother brainstormed different kinds of jobs and places to work (see the "Nine Good Jobs" sidebar). Robert's mom promised incentives to help him accomplish each step of their plan. She'd cook his favorite meal the day after he completed each step by the deadline. If he didn't make it, he would lose the use of the car for two days.

Show Him Why Work Honors God

As you guide your teen in the job-landing process, help him understand that work is more than a job. It's an opportunity to serve God. It's a way to find God's purpose for your life. It's a way to learn how to get along with people, to work as part of a team, and to take instruction from people besides parents and teachers. It's also a way to balance life—not working or playing too much, but instead blending both in proper proportions. So in addition to helping your teenagers earn their own money, guide your teens to the satisfaction of doing a job well. They'll come home proud of their efforts and pleased about learning new skills.

How can your teenagers serve God in a simple after-school job? Each action they choose can draw customers and coworkers closer to the way God wants them to live (see Matthew 5:16; 6:10). Ponder for a moment all the ways your teenager can honor God through working wholeheartedly in a part-time job (see Colossians 3:23):

- As a burger flipper, he can cook the food perfectly so a picky toddler will eat well and not throw a tantrum.
- As a greeter at a restaurant or a department store, she can cheer up a tired mother so that mother won't snap at her children.
- As a retail worker, he can help a customer feel valued so the customer won't have to be overbearing to get attention.
- At the hardware store, she can help a customer find the right pieces to repair the step so no one will trip and twist an ankle.
- On the construction site, he can watch his language to testify to the fact that girls are people, not objects to talk about crudely.
- As a janitor, he can clean the church building so well that no one is distracted from worship by spills, dust, or clutter.
- As a secretary, she can file papers carefully so the adoption goes

---

WHEN YOUR TEEN BLOWS MONEY

Let's say your teenager warms to the idea of earning his own money, but once he has a few paychecks in hand, he blows his money rather than manages it. Try actions like these:

- Stop giving your teen money. Few people mind spending someone else's money, but most people are more careful when the money they themselves earn is all the money they get.
- Declare that he can have 10 percent of the money he earns for spending and that the rest must go to pay for what he's already purchased or must be put into a bank account for job training, college tuition, or another long-term goal. Ban withdrawal access to this account.
- Don't let your teen use the things in your home that cost extra money—automobiles, cell phones, Internet service, cable television—unless he chips in to help cover the cost. However, since

through more quickly and the young child arrives sooner at his new home.

Challenge your teenager to name even more ways to minister through work and to see work as a way to honor God. Talk over each workday, inviting your teen to tell you one action she's proud of and one way she can do even better the next day to honor Christ.

SHARE IN THE TRIUMPHS

Robert's mom warned him that it might take several tries to get a job. She also warned him that he might not get the job he wanted most. But she was glad to eat her words when his job search proceeded smoothly.

---

you pay the same house payment and utility costs whether your teen lives there or not, don't charge him for those things.

- Write checks when you're giving your teen money for science lab fees, lunch tickets, art supplies, or musical instrument rentals at school so he won't be carrying cash that he might be tempted to spend.
- Suggest ways to have fun with less money: Order water in restaurants, have friends over to play board games rather than go to a movie, buy regular sunglasses rather than costly designer ones.
- Recruit someone—your spouse or a close friend—to help you not give your teen any more money.

Harsh? Not at all. Receiving an allowance is a privilege, not a right. When you change the circumstances so that your teen has no more free money to blow, he will find ways to make the money stretch. It's stewardship training.

"Mom! Where are you?" Robert called when he arrived home from his first interview.

"Back here!"

"I not only was offered the very first job I interviewed for—the one at the bookstore—but it's my first choice and I can start on Thursday if it's all right with you and Dad!"

"You're kidding?"

"Nope. You said I'd have to do two interviews before receiving an offer. But I just did one, and I got the job I wanted. Can I stop applying now?"

Robert's situation is rare, but job experiences are as varied as teenagers. Three things do remain fairly steady, however. First, once teens get to work, things tend to go well. They gear up for looking competent in front of bosses, coworkers, and customers. Second, your teen will need a little work-ethic training from you so he can honor God well at work. And third, it won't take long before the triumph of finding a job will fade into not wanting to go to work. During these struggles, keep remembering your teen's initial excitement.

After a few weeks at the bookstore, Robert came home with an intriguing statement: "Mom, you'll want to know how I managed tonight's star customer."

"What did he do?"

"It was a *she*. She came in and wanted a book on po-try."

"Po-try?"

"Yes. So I took her to our books of poems. She said, "No, no. Po-try. You know, *Po-try*, with the cookbooks! I still wasn't sure what she meant, but I took her to the cookbook section. She found what she wanted—she meant *poul*-try, a book of recipes for cooking chicken!"

"Oh, I get it. Poultry with an *l*."

"Exactly! But I didn't laugh at her. I treated her with respect like you always say to do. But I almost lost it!"

"Yep, sometimes it's hard."

"At first I thought she was just uneducated, but then I figured she might have a speech impediment. I don't think she can pronounce her l's."

"Could be. That's a very compassionate response. Whether her mispronunciation was due to a speech difficulty or not, she deserves respect."

"The other guys wanted to poke fun at her, but I wouldn't do it."

"What happened?"

"They stopped after a while."

"Good witness."

"Witness? I'm working at a bookstore, Mom. It wasn't a Bible study or anything."

"No, but you taught the Bible just as certainly. You showed what it looks like to 'clothe yourselves with compassion, kindness, humility, gentleness and patience' as it says to do in Colossians 3:12."

"I did all that?"

"Yep, you did. Compassion means to feel with someone. You felt inside what that woman might have been feeling trying to communicate what kind of book she needed. Then you let your compassion, your 'feeling with,' lead to kindness and patience."

"Cool."

"Yes, it is. The strongest Bible lessons are taught through actions. I'm proud of you, Robert."

"Thanks, Mom."

The rewards of doing a job well are evident in Robert's story. But remember the third steady principle of teenagers and work: It doesn't take long before the excitement over starting a new job fades into a dark attitude of not wanting to go to work anymore. Your teen will prefer to return to the carefree days when you supplied his monetary needs. When this happens, you'll have to hold steady.

Interestingly, Robert had balked at going to work on the very night he helped the customer find the cookbook. He had wanted to call in a substitute because he was worn out after a horrible week at school. But his mom made him go anyway. And he came home happy, full of the joy that comes from doing the right thing for the right reason. So keep on keeping on to give your teen opportunities to triumph.

The next night Robert resisted going to work once again: "Why do I have to work, Mom?" he complained. "I've already learned to appreciate money and accomplishment and all the things you told me I'd gain through a job."

"You need to work because it gives you a way to fulfill your purpose in Christ."

"By putting books on shelves?"

"That's right. You might not want to do that your whole life, but whatever job you do, you can do it for the Lord."

"If I didn't have to work, I could organize a home Bible study group. That would be something I could do for the Lord even better."

"Your working doesn't prevent that. You can host a Bible study on a different night. And because you work, you'll have money to buy snacks for the group."

"But why can't you supply the snacks? You have all kinds of money!"

"Maybe I do. Maybe I don't. The fact remains that you need spending money and money to help with college tuition. So you need to work."

"You have a good job. Why don't you just provide those things for me?"

"Because it will mean more to you if you earn it yourself."

"I promise I'll treasure what you give me just like I had earned it myself," Robert said with just a glint of teasing in his eyes.

His mom teased right back, "Sorry. Go ahead and get to work, or you'll be late."

DEVELOP A WORK ETHIC

You'll have to guide your teenager in developing his work ethic almost daily. This process won't end when he gets a job or experiences a triumph at work or hears the boss say, "Good job!" Your teen will try to convince you that he has far more important things to do than go to work. But you'll insist that he report to work as scheduled, and usually he'll come home happy a few hours later. You may also have the opposite problem—your teen wants to work so much that he's too tired for

---

WHY DOES MONEY MANAGEMENT MATTER?

Two-year-olds have it right when they insist, "Me do it!" Money management means you can do it yourself. Learning to manage money brings a number of additional benefits:

- Choosing how to spend your money means you can build the wisdom to choose how to spend your time, your energy, and your attention. Managing your own money means you build the skills to choose what to do when and with whom.
- Money management means you can pay for an item just once rather than three or four times. Buying on time incurs interest charges, which multiplies the price of the item.
- Telling yourself "no for now" means you can achieve the best later rather than settle for what is mediocre today.
- Realizing you have only so much money to spend means you'll be in control of your cash rather than allowing others to control your spending.

---

school or friends. Learning to work well, and to blend it around other aspects of life, is an ongoing process, a process many of us adults are still in the midst of.

Think of the process of developing a good work ethic as a three-legged stool that is strong and stable because it has a leg of persistence, a leg of excellence, and a leg of interest.

PERSISTENCE

Agree with your teenager that work can sometimes be monotonous and boring. Explain that the kinds of jobs he gets before graduating high school may not be the ones he wants to stay with. Shelving books isn't as interesting as writing books or designing covers for books or directing the marketing operation for a book publisher. But doing well at shelving and selling books just might provide foundational skills for becoming a better writer, designer, or marketing director. Even when earning money is enticing, staying in school means a better job for the rest of life.

EXCELLENCE

Encourage your teen to perform with excellence no matter what he does and no matter how trivial the work may seem. Explain to your teen that doing one's best honors God. He is worshiping God when he follows the path of 1 Corinthians 10:31: "So whether you eat or drink or whatever you do, do it all for the glory of God." Visit your teenager at work to catch him doing the right thing. Encourage him to brag to you about the nice things the boss says about him. Prod him to find new and better ways to organize his workspace. Agree with your teen that if he doesn't want to shelve books forever, he must choose to do well in school, to make good grades and get into a good college or trade school. Stress that trade school or college won't automatically guarantee more money, but it will open options for a wider variety of jobs.

INTEREST

Your teenager won't love his or her summer or after-school job without your showing daily interest and steady connection. Your teen will want to tell you how he is striving for excellence in his part-time job, but he'll stop if you show a lack of interest. Respond to his stories with fascination first, and save any needed correction for later. Rather than pick apart each detail to tell your teen how he might have done better, limit your suggestions to a phrase or two. Invite him to add his own ideas. Here's a conversation between Robert and his mom that included all three legs of a good work ethic (persistence, excellence, and interest):

"So you had to work nine long hours today?"

"Yeah. I not only had to get up at the crack of dawn on a Saturday, but my manager asked me to work three extra hours. Now I feel like my Saturday is shot."

"You do look tired, but there are a few good hours left yet."

"I had to receive stock, shelve books, and straighten the entire magazine section. We didn't even have many customers. It was so boring."

"I imagine so. Were there any pinpricks of light in the day?"

"Well, there were a couple of little kids who came to the children's section. I pointed them to the mystery series you used to read to us. They left really happy. And their dad mouthed a thank-you to me."

"See, you changed that dad's day. He'll now get to talk with his kids about clues and cases and keeping on until you solve the mystery."

"He'll also get to read with his kids. I would love that as a dad."

"You chose to do excellent work even in the midst of a boring day."

"I guess."

"I know you'd still rather have had more time to work on the engine you're rebuilding. But without your paycheck, you wouldn't have money to buy the parts."

"That's true, I guess."

"So your persisting through a long day meant you can go on out and work in the garage without having to earn money some other way."

"You mean I can still work on my engine even though it's this late?"

"Sure. There should be time in every day for both work and play."

ANOTHER TEEN'S STORY

There are a few highly motivated teens who can hardly wait to get a job. They may enjoy the independence that comes with work, or they may have a large-ticket item they want to purchase. Even with a self-motivated worker, however, you'll need to provide parental guidance.

REASONS TO MAKE YOUR TEENAGER WORK

Too many people believe that others owe them money, comfort, and happiness. Work shows your teenager that these commodities are built by our honest labor, not granted to us by others. Holding down an after-school job also brings these benefits:

- Doing a good job creates a strong sense of belonging and teaches important lessons about teamwork.
- Your teenager realizes that he has skills that can benefit others and that others want to recognize.
- Your teenager has an opportunity to learn how to balance her life—work, relationships, and play—all to the glory of God. She can't learn this life skill without a job, and she'll do this best with you alongside to guide her.

First, continue to teach good work ethics, reminding your teen that work is not just earning money but is meaningful activity that glorifies God. Second, refuse to allow your teen to buy a car or other big-ticket item until she has taken care of everyday expenses such as clothing and spending money. Car payments plus insurance can result in the car owning your teenager, rather than the teenager owning the car. Delaying gratification for a while can let your teen discover that materialism isn't the goal of working; taking care of daily necessities is.

Caution #1: Especially with highly motivated teens, watch that the job doesn't consume energy that is needed for schoolwork. Learning to balance time is a great benefit of having a part-time job, but keep the job demands reasonable. Working a reasonable number of hours helps students focus on school because there is less free time to waste.

Caution #2: Not all teens want or need to go to college. So see the part-time job not just as a money earner, but perhaps a door to other jobs after high school. Your teen who works in a clothing store might go on to get technical training in operating the computer system that runs the cash registers.

FIT LIFE AROUND WORK

When school let out for the summer, Robert's parents had to struggle to get him to work full-time hours during that first summer vacation. But their persistence paid off the second summer when Robert volunteered to work overtime almost every week. He enjoyed it when his boss commended his abilities, and he also liked the extra pay since he was saving up for college that fall. The main problem remaining was his claim that when he got home from work he was too tired to do his chores.

His mom had to take a deep breath and resist the urge to launch into listing all the things she does every day besides earning money. Instead, she calmly talked her son through the realities of work and life:

Jobs That Fall Short

Simply getting a job won't solve everything. Your teen must also learn a good work ethic and must discover what to do in response to those who don't show God-honoring ethics at work, such as:

- *Slacking off.* When your teen slacks off at work, gives away free food, gives portions larger than directed, or in any way delivers an effort that is less than excellent work, talk together about why this matters. Urge your teen to honor God in even the tiniest details with questions like: "How can you obey all Ten Commandments at work?" (e.g., giving away free food is a form of stealing), "How is God honored or dishonored in this?" "How do the portion rules keep the business afloat?"

- *Showing up late.* Giving a full hour's work for a full hour's pay is a way to tell the truth, and it's a good witness to an employer. Though your teen's employer may dock pay for showing up late, you may also want to impose a penalty when your teen fails to arrive on time. By the same token, give bonuses for arriving early with the reward of more time with friends on the weekend. To demonstrate the importance of punctuality, invite your teen to talk about her reactions when people are late for dates or for other important appointments.

- *Unsafe conditions.* Not all the problems will originate with your teen. The boss may put your child's safety at risk by asking that he close up late at night when he is the only employee in the store. If this happens, use community rules as your ally. Your teen could ask to leave work early enough to be home by your community's curfew. Or impose a family curfew that your teens must meet.

As with other tricky job situations, you may have to help your teen get a different job if this one requires too many compromises.

- *Unreasonable managers.* Your teen's manager may want your teen to work too many weekday hours. This may happen simply because your teen does not stand up for himself. So teach the "I wish I could…" approach. If the boss asks, "Can you come in two extra days this week?" your son can say, "I wish I could, but I need to limit my work to fifteen hours to keep up with school." Other times the boss simply adds your son to the schedule. Once again, respectful repetition can help: "I'd like to work more, but I must limit it to fifteen hours a week. Which days do you most need me here?"

- *Unethical practices.* Your teenage daughter may be asked to ride alone in a car with a male boss or work late with a male boss who makes sexual advances. Instruct her not to do this, stressing that her safety is much more important than money. Assure your teen that if she finds herself in a compromising situation, she can call anytime and you will come. Urge her to get a different job if her boss does this more than once, if her boss asks her to steal or lie, or if other unethical situations exist.

If circumstances don't change and it's necessary to seek other employment, make sure your teen has another job lined up before quitting the first one. Teens like the heady power of saying "I quit!" but it's easier to get another job while still employed. The exception is when your teen is in immediate physical, sexual, or ethical danger.

"Robert, it's more fun to do the kind of work that earns money."

"I guess."

"But it's definitely not much fun doing work that earns no money."

"Now that I'm earning money, I'm not doing that unpaid stuff anymore. And I don't receive an allowance any longer, so I don't need to do chores."

"It's not quite that simple. Because we live in a family, there are still home chores to do: laundry and cooking, yard work and repairs, errand running and grocery shopping."

"If it takes all that to live in a family, I'm going to live alone!"

"If you live alone, you have to do *all* of those things by yourself."

"Ugh!"

"That's right. Living in a family means we can share the chores."

"I'll take the errand running. I like to drive."

"I may take you up on that. But there are other chores that have to be done every day. I need you to take some of those."

"I'll bring in the mail."

"And you'll take out the trash."

"Yuck! I hate that smelly trash can."

"So does everybody else. These tasks are called *chores* because they're no fun. We've got to divide and conquer."

"Well, on days I don't work, I guess I don't mind. But when I have homework and work on the same day, I don't have time for chores."

"Gotta make time, Robert. That's the way things work."

Was Robert's mom too rough on him? Not at all. We all have to find time for chores after a grueling day, even when we bring work home or have schoolwork to do. Robert has to live as a participating family member, just like the rest of the family. As his mom refuses to spoil him, he learns to buckle down and do what needs to be done. Refuse to let your teenager assume that others are there to wait on him.

WILL HE EVER GET OUT ON HIS OWN?

Independence takes time to learn. Teach these skills so your teen can become a happily independent adult:

- *Earn your own money.* No matter how many mission trips, school demands, or social commitments your teen already has, insist that she get a part-time job. The two most effective ways to do this are (1) to stop giving your teen any spending money, gasoline money, mission-trip money, or clothing, and (2) to impose a deadline for finding employment.

- *Manage your money.* During your teen's junior or senior year, go with him to open a checking account, perhaps an account that also has a check card. Then take a year to supervise transactions and work on balancing the checkbook. Good accounting skills take practice.

- *Do your own laundry.* Announce this new responsibility the first week of your teen's senior year. Show him how to use the washer and dryer, suggest setting a beeper on his watch to remember permanent press, and then refuse to bail him out when life gets crazy. (When he is living in another city or at college, you can't bail him out.)

- *Show receipts.* To get reimbursed for phone bills, school fees, and other expenses you cover, your teen must show you a written receipt. It's not just good business; it's what he'll have to do for his future employers.

- *Follow the rules.* Whether living in an apartment, a dorm, or your house, there are always rules to be followed. Let your teen practice rule-following with house rules like church every Sunday morning, chores before going out, and letting you know where he's going when he leaves the house.

MOVE PAST THE DRUDGERY

Work gets a bad reputation in our culture. To free your teen from this sense of dread, deliberately focus on the clear benefits that God has built into work:

- Work gives me a place in society: "I do carpentry well so my neighbors can have sturdy houses."
- Work gives me a sense of purpose for the day: "Today I framed windows so children can look outside and appreciate God's creation"
- Work provides opportunities to show God's love: "Today the other carpenters and I worked faster and better than we ever had. It was a great day of teamwork because I looked for ways to help the other guys instead of just looking out for myself" (see Philippians 2:4).
- Work lets me learn life skills such as love, joy, peace, patience, kindness, goodness, faithfulness, gentleness, and self-control: "It took a God-sized batch of self-control to show patience to my crabby supervisor today. I think I finally won him over though."

ACTION STEPS

Work provides a platform for honoring God, a confidence borne from competence, a chance to triumph over adversity, people skills, lessons in money management and taking instructions from people other than family, and more. Refuse to let your teenager miss these success markers by giving him money he hasn't worked for. Instead, show him how to earn and manage his own money.

What Scripture says: "Whatever you do, work at it with all your heart, as working for the Lord, not for men" (Colossians 3:23).

Explain to your teen: "Work is not punishment but a way to find your purpose in life. No matter what your job is, you can serve God through it. You can cheer people up as they come through your checkout line. You can care for coworkers as you labor together over a hot grill. You can smile at the workers that no one else pays attention to. Let your job be a challenge to serve Christ well."

[9]

MY TEENAGER IS SO MOODY

I DON'T RECOGNIZE HIM

SHOW YOUR TEEN HOW TO POINT INTENSE
FEELINGS TOWARD GOOD ACTION

David had been griping all afternoon. When his dad asked about his bad mood, the teenager crankily demanded that he just be left alone.

"David, you can be sad and mad, but you have to express your feelings respectfully."

"I'm too upset right now to talk," David said as he started to leave the room.

"That may well be, but sometimes you have to talk anyway. I'll give you ten minutes to calm down, and we can start again."

"I won't be ready then either."

"Well, if you can't talk then, we'll have to look at some consequences."

"You're going to punish me for being in a bad mood? I can't help my emotions!"

"You can't help the feeling, but you can control what you do with it."

"I can handle this myself!"

"Because we're family, we go through life together. God has given us emotions, and when one of them rears its head, God will show us what to do about it."

"Then let me and God handle this. It's none of your business!"

"It became my business when you chose to gripe and then yell at me."

"Why can't you just leave me alone?"

Teenagers like David have gained a bad reputation for being moody. Sometimes teenagers *are* moody, but mostly they're just real people with real feelings that are very new to them. The feelings themselves may not be new—they've felt happiness or sadness before—but the *intensity* of the feelings is stunningly new. Without warning, any sensation can become painfully intense, and just about the time teens get used to one feeling, a different one charges in to take its place. It's like riding a roller coaster with nothing to hold them in the seat. Teens feel jerked around and desperate for any security that will hold them tight.

So hug your teen with words, and then hug him again with actions. This gives him the safety bars he needs—tools that will help him identify what he's feeling and discover what to do about it.

DIAGNOSE THE FEELING

Since David's feelings were so intense, his dad gave him the full ten minutes to calm down. When the time was up, he went to David's room and asked him to come to the kitchen table. His dad began their conversation again with renewed calmness.

"David, feelings are confusing and powerful, but they are not our bosses. They are arrows that point us toward good action, not dictators that push us to fight. God created our feelings, and he wants to show you what to do with this one."

"Maybe things in life are bad and I just feel sad about it," David responded, his mood not much improved.

"Sometimes that's exactly what you should do. Taking time to be sad can energize you to take action against the cause of your sadness. Or sometimes you just need some sleep. But you also have to talk to me about what's making you sad."

"But it's my life!"

"And sharing your life with your family gives you more power to handle it."

"Well, I don't know what I'm sad about. Okay, are you happy now?"

"Watch it, David. You must choose a respectful tone of voice."

"I don't have to do anything."

"No, you don't. But when consequences come, you'll wish you had chosen respect. One more rude comment and it's a five-dollar fine."

"You can't fine me for being sad," he said with just as much rudeness.

"I just did. Five dollars, please."

"But..."

"Take a deep breath before you lose another five dollars."

David remained silent, but sparks flew from his eyes. His dad paused, then ventured, "You were sad, and now you're mad. Those feelings are fine. But ugly outbursts are not. The Bible clearly tells us to be

---

FIVE WAYS TO DEFUSE EMOTION OVERLOAD

1. Take a nap.
2. Take a walk or get some exercise.
3. Take someone with you on a walk and talk it out. Once you've aired things out, blow away the chaff.
4. Sit down with a good book, some good music, or an encouraging movie.
5. Write, draw, paint, or make a list. Put onto paper how you feel and why.

---

angry without sin. After this interchange I'm angry too. So I'm having to watch what I say. That's why I'm taking a deep breath and lowering my tone. Likewise, I expect you to talk calmly about your feelings. As we talk, we will find solutions. Once you've told me three things about this feeling, you can have some time alone."

An hour later, after sitting at the table in silence, David asked for a notepad. He wrote down his feelings, explaining that the very person he'd been trying to befriend had turned on him and started a vicious rumor. David felt betrayed because he went out of his way to stand up for this guy when no one else would. But the boy had sided with a group that called David a loser. They even stuck a sign on his locker to that effect.

David's dad read the note and felt a combination of sadness and fury. "David, my first reaction is to go show those guys what it feels like to be a loser. But I know that's not the action God's pushing me toward. I'm also really sad. Let's think through this a bit while we play basketball. Are you up for a little one-on-one?"

During the basketball game, they worked out a game plan. David would say hello to this boy, but he wouldn't pursue any conversation. This would serve two purposes: (1) It would confuse the boy, because David was continuing to be nice in spite of the nasty rumor, and (2) it would help protect David from further rumors because he wasn't taking vindictive action against the boy. They agreed this would take much more manhood than picking a fight with the guy.

This type of exchange with your teen might take a few hours or even a few days. But each time an emotion surfaces, persist until the two of you can figure out what to do about it. Even if your son is upset about a here-today-gone-tomorrow occurrence, it's still critical that he establish the habit of working with family members to talk through and walk through each time together. This chapter includes sidebars that address each of the eight most common teen emotions, both the welcome emotions and the troubling ones. These include pride, love, sadness, anger, fear, shyness, embarrassment, and happiness. As you help your teen work through his feelings, remember to be just as responsive to his positive emotions as you are to the negative ones (see Romans 12:15).

TIPS FOR HANDLING PRIDE, BOTH GOOD AND BAD

Pride has a positive side when it's a feeling that follows a hard-earned accomplishment. But it also has a darker side that can disrupt relationships and hurt others. So celebrate good pride and ban bad pride with actions like these:

- Recognize pride in a job well done as good and godly pride (Colossians 3:23). Commend your teen for diligent effort. Celebrate by going out to eat when your teen does something well— holds his temper when he's taunted at school, makes a good solid B on a difficult test, shows a good attitude at home after an exhausting mission trip.
- Identify in yourself the stubborn don't-confuse-me-with-the-facts-because-I've-already-made-up-my-mind pride before it leads to destruction (see Proverbs 16:18). Help your teen do the same.
- Compassionately but firmly identify a haughty spirit in your teen: "Honey, you're taking a stand that dares anyone to help you or correct you. You're setting yourself up for excruciating pain. Please let God open your heart to receive help from others."
- Together with your teen, identify words or tones that stir up stubborn pride on your part or your teen's part. Then name ways to avoid going down those paths.

Take the Direct Approach

Dealing directly with emotions is volatile. It can make even the calmest parent lose it and yell at a teen. It can make a placid teen claw like a cornered cougar. But taking the difficult step of directness will drain away all the destruction; it also prevents even more disastrous explosions down the road. At the very least, it keeps your irreplaceably precious teenager from suffering in lonely silence. So be the adult and take the direct approach.

First, calm yourself down. Then plug into God's power source and invite a Holy Spirit–inspired dose of understanding. Skip ahead to chapter 10, page 203, and commit to practice the "Five Ways to Keep Things Calm" sidebar.

Teens are convinced they can handle life on their own, or perhaps in tandem with God. David told his dad that he and God could take care of his sadness. And when you think about it, doesn't he have a good point?

No.

If David could grasp God's showing him how to diagnose his feeling and decide what to do about it, the teen would already have solved the problem. God put kids into families so parents can equip them to grow to maturity. One aspect of maturity is learning how to diagnose the cause of our feelings and then prescribe what to do about them. So let God work through you to teach your teens about emotions and what to do with them. No one book can address every emotion your teens will face. So customize the principles in this chapter to fit your teenager's particular needs. Here are two guiding principles that apply maturity to a teenager's intense emotions:

- Emotions are arrows, not bosses. Our feelings don't control us; they point us to a constructive action that we need to take.

- The two biggest temptations with emotions are (1) to become totally piggish by demanding that everyone else cater to our current feeling, or (2) to try to ignore and push away the emotions. Don't give in to either temptation. No matter what the

FIVE PHRASES AND FIVE ACTIONS THAT SHOW LOVE

Teens need to hear and see regular expressions of love. So demonstrate your love through these actions.

1. Listen every day with rapt attention to the events of your teen's day.
2. Be there to watch your teen lead worship, play a ball game, march in the band, present his art project—whatever he does publicly.
3. Spend time alone with each of your teens every week. Go out to eat; work on a puzzle together; take a drive. Let this be a time your teen can count on having your undivided attention.
4. Practice what you preach: Act with honor; tell the truth; be on time; call when you'll be late; value people; evaluate relationships before investing too deeply.
5. Open your home so your teen's friends can come and be loved by you and your teen. But always assure your teen privately that he is number one to you.

After putting your love into action, make sure you follow up those actions with words. Here are five sincere expressions that mean a lot to your teenager.

1. "You're brilliant."
2. "You do that so well."
3. "Can I sit by you?"
4. "I'm going out. Wanna go with me?"
5. "Your thoughts and feelings matter to me."

emotion, there are things you and your teen can do to right the wrong, to solve the problem, or to move on through the pain to the good on the other side.

This process is never easy. Most parents would much rather let their teens stay in their rooms until they get the ranting and raving out of their systems, or until the sadness is over. But when parents take a hands-off approach, their teens get jerked around and bruised by that emotion as well as all the emotions that come after it.

So determine to be the person your teenagers can safely bounce against until they can harness and drive their own emotions. If you don't secure your teen, a wayward girlfriend or another companion who doesn't have your teen's best interest at heart will gladly lead him down another path to supposed comfort. And your teen will end up more miserable than ever.

DECIDE THE ACTION

The weird part about emotions is that each one can mean so many things. Simple sadness can mean something sad has happened. It can mean your teen has done something wrong that she doesn't want you to know about. It can mean your teen is out of fuel and needs sleep. It can mean fear of a present or future enemy. Or it can mean a number of other things are going on. So you have to walk with your teen through the muck of confusion until you both find the reason for the feeling. Only then can you discover what to do about it.

Pain is not something to coddle or fuss over. But it's also not something to ignore. It's something to address. Find out what's causing the feelings, figure out what to do about it, and then do what's needed. Finally, move back to happiness.

Walk backward until you have diagnosed the cause. But first, take care of a little attitude adjustment. When your teen mopes around and feels sorry for herself, your first reaction may be that she is just plain selfish. You want her to snap out of it. But you miss something when you jump to conclusions about your teen's moods. Rachel's pain might be selfish, or it might be well warranted. The key is what she does in response to it. So rather than conclude that your teen is being selfish, show her how *not* to be selfish. Here's how it happened for Rachel and her mother:

"Rachel, you seem extra sad today."

"Yeah. Just the blues I guess."

"It could be. But the blues usually have a cause. You left this morning in a chipper mood. Did something happen to make you sad?"

"I don't know."

"Well, tell me about your day."

"My math teacher was gone, so we had boring worksheets rather than his usual motion-math demonstration. English was a reading day. The other classes were just average. Maybe the problem is that nothing really happened."

"No zip in the day, huh?"

"None."

"How are your friends doing?"

"I didn't get to see Gretchen. Benjamin spent most of his time talking to his guy friends. I didn't really have much of a conversation with anyone."

"So you were lonely too?"

"Yeah, I guess that's the word for it."

"Some days are like that."

"I feel like I've had a month of days like that."

"That would make anybody sad. The good news is that you don't have to settle for being sad or lonely. You can be the one to seek Gretchen out and to ask Benjamin about that test he's been worrying about."

"What good will that do?"

"As you go out of your way to talk with people, you'll experience the exhilaration of connection. You'll feel less lonely and more energized to manage a boring class. Then even if your teacher gives a long, boring lecture, your zip will prompt you to listen for interesting details in what he is saying."

Rachel looked at her mom disbelieving, and she rolled her eyes. "You're telling me that starting a couple of conversations can transform a boring lecture?"

"That's exactly what I'm saying. Because every experience requires someone to initiate it and someone to respond, you can have an impact from either side. Your interested response helps you see something interesting, even in a not-so-well-presented lecture. You can't change your teacher. But you can change you."

"If you say so."

Your own teen may not immediately act on your suggestions, and the first suggestions you make may not work. But keep trying until the two of you find the reason for the emotion and the actions that God wants your teenager to take. This happens over a matter of days rather than a single conversation.

The next day Rachel came home with some news. "I tried your talking prescription, Mom."

"And?"

"Gretchen looked surprised that I actually sought her out."

"Cool."

"And when I asked Ben how things were going, he said, 'Thanks for asking, Rachel.' I guess taking initiative really does make a difference." Rachel bounded up the stairs to tackle her homework. She was clearly happy, and so was her mom.

Your overall goal is not to make your teenager happy—that's a selfish focus that teaches your teen that she's the center of the universe.

Instead, the goal is to show her how to respond to each emotion in God-honoring ways. Your role is to move her past being confused over her feelings and move her toward the solution to those feelings.

Rachel's mom found that important middle ground between walking on eggshells and ignoring all of her daughter's emotions. Walking on eggshells gives the emotion disproportionate power to control the situation and your teenager. Suppressing or explaining away all emotions ignores what God might be trying to communicate through the emotion—to reach out, to solve a problem, to make a move. Walk your teenager all the way through to the solution to be found on the other side.

FIND A SOLUTION TOGETHER

Throughout the process of teaching your teen to manage emotions, let her know why her emotions make sense and then show her what to do about them. For example, when the World Trade Center towers and the Pentagon were attacked by terrorists using commercial airliners, and when a fourth plane crashed before it could reach its target on September 11, 2001, it made perfect sense to be angry. Thousands of innocent people were killed in acts of deliberate aggression.

The wrong that needed to be righted was terrorism fed by governments, by money, and by cruelly masterminded evil. In the wake of such horror, there were tangible things teenagers could do to help, such as raise money for relief efforts, build relationships that overcome hate, write letters to military personnel, and pray for our nation's leaders. In powerfully painful situations like this, make sure your teen knows that her emotions are well founded. Help your teenagers understand how emotions serve as fuel that empowers them to act on God's behalf. We Christians do this well with upbeat and welcome emotions. It's sadness and anger that we Christians struggle with.

Why is there so much sadness and anger in teen experiences? Because life is hard. Even their very best efforts sometimes go unrewarded, beloved friends and relatives are stricken with serious illnesses, bad people win over good ones, and the mean kids at school get all the accolades and the good dates. Life isn't fair, and it hurts like crazy. Add to that the intensity of emotion caused by the hormones that are transforming your offspring from a child into an adult, and you have the recipe for shaky days.

The compassion and idealism that is characteristic of teenagers also adds emotion to their worlds. Rather than downplay this, harness it. Recognize this passion as one of your teen's very best features. Even when compassion for homeless families plunges your teen into the depths of despair, affirm her courage to empathize with other people, and then equip your teen to channel the energy behind her passion to the right places. She may want to give her Saturdays to Habitat for Humanity or another group that builds reasonably priced housing. With your care and guidance, you and your teen can enjoy stability, even with passionate idealism and the agony of real life. You can show your teen how to manage and make the most of her intense emotions (see Romans 12:15).

Here's how Rachel's mom directed her daughter after a tragic auto accident injured a close friend and her brother.

"It's just not fair, Mom. Kathleen never hurt anybody in her life. Why was she the one who had to become paralyzed?" Rachel asked, agonizing over her friend's injuries.

"She didn't have to be," her mom told her. "God doesn't plan or cause things like this. The other driver chose to run a red light, and now Kathleen and her brother are in the hospital."

"But it's not fair!"

"You're right about that. There's nothing fair or right or good about this situation."

"I just don't know what to do."

"The best thing is to do something practical for Kathleen. What if we get a bunch of little presents and wrap one for every day she'll be in the hospital? Then she can open one every morning and have something to look forward to."

"That would be a whole lot more fun than just waking up in a hospital bed every day. Do you think we should number them?"

"Sure. Even making a game out of it would be fun. You could put a clue inside each gift that gives hints about what the next day's present will be. There's always something you can do to help someone who is hurting."

"What about Kathleen's brother? They say Tyrone will be in a coma for weeks. He can't open gifts."

FIVE WAYS TO SHARE SADNESS

During times of sadness, you may first notice your teenager acting crabby. Peek behind the outward grouchiness to see the sadness lurking in the shadows. Identify it. Then coax it out with these questions and actions.

1. "Tell me three things about what happened. Then I'll let you be. I'm not trying to pry, but when families share sadness, it becomes more manageable."
2. "Your sadness makes sense because…"
3. "What do you think we should do now that this has happened?"
4. "Is this a sadness we can do something about, or do we just have to let it go?" (If a friend has been in a car accident, your teen can provide practical help, but if she was cut from the team, she'll have to let it go and join the intramural league.)
5. Sometime during the sad event, just take time to be sad together. You might want to cry, hug, or just sit together quietly.

"Maybe not, but you could make him a tape telling him the things you appreciate about him."

"Do you think he can hear it?"

"Maybe not, but it's worth a try. Even if he can't hear it, his visitors will hear it. It will encourage them."

"Okay. Where's the tape recorder?"

With a bit of listening and a few simple suggestions, Rachel's mom moved her daughter from the despair of sadness to caring acts in response to her sadness. Rachel now had practical actions to take in expressing her sadness over her injured friends, actions that would make a real difference in real lives. Purposeful action is the key to helping teenagers manage their emotions.

It All Comes at Once

In the aftermath of an incident like a friend being injured in a car crash, your teenager will not have the luxury of feeling only the emotions concerning her friend's condition. She'll have those emotions *plus* all her other everyday feelings and confusion. So give her extra strategies to handle it all, being aware that emotions are arrows, not dictators. They don't control us, but they do point us in the direction of needed action.

If your teen has a physical, emotional, or health concern that gives him extra obstacles to overcome, he is in a similar situation. He does not have the luxury of dealing only with those challenges. He has that *plus* his regular everyday emotions and obstacles of life. So give him extra steadying, extra tools, extra energy. Don't expect others to indulge him because of the disability, the disease, or even the extra stress he's facing. That's spoiling, and nobody likes being around a spoiled person. Certainly it's unfair that your teen has to manage not only the everyday obstacles of life, but also the crisis or the disability or the disease he's struggling to overcome. He doesn't get to replace the regular challenges of life with this other big one. He has to do *both*. It's not fair, but that's the way it is. So refuse to saddle him with a third obstacle—self-centeredness. Instead, equip him to clear *all* the hurdles in life, the everyday issues in addition to the special ones that are peculiar to his life circumstance.

As you bolster your teen to respond well to emotions, recognize that emotions are not something to be experienced and then set aside so we can move on. They are signals pointing us toward God's next step. So follow the arrows. Warn your teen against just acting on his immediate feelings. When your teen hears of his friend's cancer diagnosis, he may feel like punching a hole in the wall, but the broken hand that results testifies to the foolishness of that response. Instead, help your teen channel his sadness and anger into making a donation to cancer research, perhaps specified for his friend's clinical trial. Your teen might go a step further by committing to major in premed and eventually to become an oncologist who researches a cancer cure.

Look with God's perspective toward the next step and then follow in that path. In Rachel's case, her sadness pointed her toward doing something concrete to help her injured friends. After listing several possibilities, she made some cool wheelchair clothing for Kathleen so she could feel more stylish when she returned to school. Since Kathleen was missing her classmates, Rachel organized a group of friends to write personal notes so Kathleen would have a new letter to read every day for three weeks. In addition, she became a caring listener for Kathleen. She listened to her friend's fears, letting her talk and avoiding trying to give quick advice to "solve" her hurt. Rachel recorded friends at school saying hello and giving news. She also asked Kathleen to jot down her own needs and wishes and then found ways to supply what she needed. These wishes included someone to get homework assignments, her favorite fruit smoothie, and a specific stuffed animal.

When Sadness Isn't the Problem

Fifteen-year-old David, whose dad helped him work through a bad mood earlier in this chapter, is ordinarily an easygoing guy. He doesn't go too high or too low. But when he becomes angry, his parents steer clear of their son. He yells, hurls accusations, and slams doors. His parents are disturbed by these eruptions, but they don't know what to do other than to let him rant until he's finished.

Steering clear of an angry teenager may be the easiest path, but it's definitely not the best one. David's anger is as frightening to him as it is to his parents. He needs someone to provide harnesses that can corral his fiery feelings, and his parents are the ones to supply these harnesses.

Interestingly, David's even temperament may be one of his worst enemies. He may hold in his emotions until they build up and erupt in a destructive outburst. As with parenting our teens through any emotion, the solution to explosive anger is more involved than a single conversation or two. David's parents need to guide their son to vent his feelings one at a time rather than wait until the pressure builds into a confusing mass of messy passions. Venting feelings as they occur, rather than letting them accumulate, is a habit that will take continual development. A good time to start guiding a teenager on channeling his outbursts is when he's feeling a bit remorseful after an episode of angry ranting. That's when David's dad decided to talk about the situation.

"David, your anger got the best of you last night, didn't it."

"Yep."

"Pretty scary, huh?"

"Well, it kinda was. I always thought of anger as losing control. But when I was in my room kicking the bedframe, I felt more than just anger. I also was feeling a ton of fear."

FIVE ACTIONS TO ADDRESS ANGER

Walking with our teens through their emotions can be heart wrenching; that's why so many parents push their teens away with too-easy answers. But this does not please God. Nor does it follow the leading of God's arrows. Instead of quick answers, give solid help by finding the practical action that offers a real solution.

1. Help your son or daughter recognize anger as a good thing, an indicator that a wrong needs to be righted. Then help your teen learn to express anger without hurting herself or someone else (see Ephesians 4:26).

2. Direct your teen to do something physical to burn off the destructive energy of anger—walk, shoot baskets, punch a punching bag or pillow, chop wood. If it helps, join your teen in an activity. But caution him against driving or joining in competitive play when he's angry.

3. As your teen works off the energy of anger, remind her to talk with God to find out the reasons behind her anger. Asking for God's help goes a long way toward solving the current cause of anger.

4. If the situation can be fixed, help your teen take appropriate action. Is he mad about someone being treated unjustly? Encourage him to deliberately treat that person fairly and motivate others to do the same.

5. If the situation can't be fixed, you can still help your teenager take effective action. Has a relative died? Do something practical for that relative's family to help them walk through this painful time.

"I know what you mean. Anger is one of the ways we express fearful feelings."

"I never thought of it that way before."

"Sadness also comes along with anger."

"Sadness too? Well, thinking about almost failing that test is what set me off. I studied and studied and still made a D."

"That's the funny thing about anger. It can erupt over the least little thing. Just one tiny thought can lead to an eruption."

"That's for sure. I'm so ashamed of spewing those accusations at you. And kicking the bedframe was pretty childish."

"Better than the wall," his dad said half jokingly.

"Well, having to pay for getting the wall repaired last time cured me of that. But kicking things is still hard on my foot, even with my work boots on."

"I imagine so."

"So what do I do, Dad?"

"Well, instead of letting your anger erupt, express the bits of feeling as each one comes. When you're upset and building toward anger, tell me about it. We'll go for a walk or play basketball or ride bikes until the energy behind that anger is spent. When you're afraid, bring it up so we can find a solution. When you're happy, go ahead and let me know so we can celebrate."

"Sometimes I just don't want to talk about it. I'm embarrassed that I almost failed the test."

"I hate failing at work as much as you do when you fail a test. Besides the fact that those emotions are prickly to talk about, our society prizes men who hold in their emotions. So it's a bit weird for us, as guys, to talk about this stuff."

"That's for sure."

"As Christians, though, we can rise above the weirdness in society. We can imitate Jesus, who wept and raged and even showed his fear."

"I never thought about that. But I guess he did cry and stuff."

"Yep, and when the friends of Lazarus saw Jesus cry, they said, 'See how he loved him.' Jesus' tears were an indicator of love, not of weakness."

"And he got mad at the moneychangers in the temple."

"Righteous anger that led to stopping a wrong."

FIVE POSITIVE RESPONSES TO FEAR

Fear frequently accompanies sadness and anger; at other times it occurs on its own. You can guide your teenager through fear with steps like these:

1. Recognize fear as a helpful emotion that guides us away from danger.

2. Together put the fear into specific words. The generalized fear of "I feel scared at school" becomes the specific "What if someone pulls out a gun and starts shooting and I don't know where to run and I get hit by a bullet?"

3. Offer helpful advice: "You can run in a zigzag, drop to the ground when you hear popping sounds, and pray 'God, which way should I turn?'"

4. Turn fear into action: Ask the principal for more detailed safety checks at school; be respectful toward everyone so no one would want to shoot you; report anything suspicious; stay aware of your surroundings.

5. Don't minimize fear. A minor fear such as being afraid to talk with people may seem less important than getting shot, but it can be just as damaging to your teenager. It keeps your teen from forming friendships and from living out the spiritual gifts that God has given her. So equip her to fight off loneliness with the four steps above. Also, assign her a talking skill to practice each day (see the "Five Solutions to Shyness" sidebar later in this chapter).

"But when did he show fear?"

"He was afraid of the cross."

"Well, nails through your feet and wrists would hurt!"

"Yep, his fears made sense. So he talked to God about them."

"I figured God cared about my thoughts, but not my feelings."

"He's the Creator of both. So he wants to show you how to manage both your ideas and your feelings, including your anger."

"That's good, because I could use a little help."

"Me, too, Son. Me, too."

When your teenager unleashes an outburst of pent-up emotion, communicate clearly that he can, and he must, manage his emotions. Our feelings don't control us; we control them with God's power. Also communicate that there are more than two options. Rather than hold emotions in or spew them out, there's an effective middle ground that lets the emotions carry out their intended purpose. Once again, this path is to follow God's arrows to the action that's needed.

LET'S CHANGE OUR REPUTATION

As you guide your teen through sadness, fear, and anger, recognize that Christians tend to deal with these emotions very poorly. We wrongly try to push them away as signs of a lack of faith. In reality, sadness, fear, and anger can be expressions of faith, declarations that as we bring our feelings to God, he can show us what to do about them. Ideally we should weep over what makes God sad, our rage should match the wrath of God, and our fear should lead to concrete actions that address unjust circumstances. For instance, the fear of being lonely can lead a teenager to learn how to initiate conversations. Fear of school shootings can lead to protection, to legislation, to responsibility, and to other actions that make everyone safer. Anger over racism can lead a teen to form friendships with people of a different ethnic heritage.

Please take note: When your teenager is under extra stress, resist the temptation to assume that because he has so much stress he doesn't have to handle his emotions. When your teenager has soccer practice, a church meeting, three tests the next day, and a major problem with a friend, he'll be a little testy. He'll want to be excused from his home chores, and he'll use all the pressure he's under as an excuse to snap at his siblings. But because there's never a good excuse for rudeness or self-centeredness, insist that he find a way to manage his feelings anyway. This is where faith makes a noticeable difference in our behavior. This is where we rise above our circumstances to say the kind thing, do the right thing, and manage the pressure without exploding. If your teen doesn't learn these faith expressions, he will become an adult who is kind only when it's convenient or who will expect to feel good all the time (and may use alcohol or another drug to achieve that state). Self-control is not an extra burden. It is a power giver. And it's a fruit of the Holy Spirit (see Galatians 5:22-23).

FIVE SOLUTIONS TO SHYNESS

If your teenager struggles with shyness, provide these assignments to teach him how to talk with people. Each task is a little more difficult than the one before it. As he masters one skill, move to the next level of difficulty while continuing to practice the former.

1. Say hello to at least two people today.
2. Give at least two people a compliment, such as "I like your shirt."
3. Remember what someone talked about and ask about it the next day.
4. Ask at least two people a question that invites them to talk. Stick around long enough to hear their answer.
5. Invite someone over or call that person on the telephone to catch up on his or her life.

EMPOWER WITH YOUR PRESENCE

Just being around you will give your teenager power to handle the easy and the hard of life, the happy and the sad. But in that process, tackle your teen's embarrassment. Refuse to believe the rumors that teenagers don't want to go out with family and don't want to do vacations. Most public places are well-suited for family togetherness. There are certain places that are definitely teen turf—the front lawn at school where kids hang out, the youth rows at church, and other select spots where kids gather. But you and your teenagers can share the overwhelming majority of places and spaces. Your teen may buck, but overcome any resistance by demonstrating your desire to spend significant time with your teen. Here's how Rachel's dad approached it:

"Hey, wanna go out for an omelet?"

"Dad, you know Justin works there!"

"Oh yeah. Well, you pick the restaurant. I don't care where we eat, just as long as we eat together."

"You are so mushy, Dad."

"That's my job. To act mushy and to embarrass my kids. How am I doing so far?"

"Too well!"

"So where are we going?"

"Do you promise to behave if we go to the pancake house and get an omelet?"

"Well, which rules do I have to obey?"

"No singing. No gesturing or pointing at Justin, if he's at work today. No being superfriendly with complete strangers. And you have to sit quietly and calmly."

"I have to remember four rules?"

"Want me to make it five?" Rachel teased.

"No, better leave it at four. I can probably keep track of four."

"Well, I'll go with you then."

"Good! Go tell Mom we want to take her out for brunch!"

Rachel's dad did a great job of using lighthearted but serious teasing to connect with his daughter. He acknowledged the embarrassment that sometimes occurs because teens want to be seen as independently

---

FIVE ACTIONS FOR SURVIVING EMBARRASSMENT

1. Recognize that when your teen is embarrassed by something you do or say, it doesn't mean your teen hates you. It means your teen wants to be seen independently as a lovable person rather than as an extension of you.

2. Let your teen approve your outfits. Your shorts and flip-flops may spark major embarrassment if you're seen by your daughter's friends. So slap on jeans and tennis shoes if it makes your teen more comfortable.

3. Act discreetly in public. Don't shout your teen's name or call out "Love you, sweetie!" Let your teen make the rules for when and where to speak when you're out in public together.

4. Insist that your teen come along on family trips and local outings. You'll end up making memories that your teen will enjoy. Pick places that let you talk and create your own fun, rather than theme parks or other places that provide ready-made entertainment. Take lots of photos and tell lots of stories afterward. The bonds built will bolster your teen for emotion management and for true enjoyment of life.

5. Invite your teenager to tell you about embarrassing moments that have nothing to do with you—like walking into the wrong bathroom at church. Then you can agonize together.

---

likable human beings. They want to be loved for who they are, not for whose child they are. But teenagers still want to be cherished as an irreplaceable part of a loving family. They crave that loving togetherness.

And that's an emotion worth working toward.

Don't Forget to Enjoy Your Teenager

Your teen's link with you is essential for keeping her grounded. So lovingly and deliberately invest in your teen by sharing her emotions. As parents, our first impulse is to assure our hurting teen that things will work out. But wishing away the suffering doesn't alleviate the pain and sadness. And as we know, some things *won't* work out. So agree with your teen that what happened really does matter. Then find the action that helps, communicating that God answers prayers through human hands. Look the emotion directly in the face to find out three things:

- Why does it make sense to feel this way?
- What wrong needs to be righted? What unfairness needs to be opposed? What pain needs to be alleviated?
- What should I do now that I understand the situation better?

Then take the appropriate actions.

When we think of common teenage emotions we think of the sad, mad, and frustrating ones. But there are just as many positive, optimistic, ecstatic feelings to share. So in the middle of all the guiding and teaching about emotions, don't forget to simply enjoy your teenagers. No one whoops with the enthusiasm of a teenager. No one decides that life has never ever been this wonderful like a teenager. Participate gladly in the exuberance of your very precious son or daughter.

Work hard at building a foundation of family happiness that gives your teenager the power he or she needs to make it through the rougher emotions of life. Then you can show your teen how to consider the needs and feelings of others even when she's mad or sad or angry. It will exhaust you, but don't give up. She needs you. And right around the corner from a time of difficult emotions will be a time of great delight.

Learn to view yourself as a teacher of emotions, not a hard taskmaster. Slowly but certainly your teenager will develop a pattern of walking through the disappointing events of her day until she finds the best solution. That's when triumph returns.

FIVE WAYS TO CELEBRATE HAPPINESS

1. Invite your teen to tell you every detail of her good news. Few can resist telling good news to a parent who really wants to hear.

2. Be willing to be silly—whoop, dance, hug, giggle. Rejoice however you and your teen most enjoy.

3. Affirm the wise things your teen did to bring about this happiness. When parents point out a teen's good actions, the teen is better equipped to repeat those good actions in the future. "Honey, your commitment to maintaining high standards in dating resulted in this really fine guy asking you out." "All your studying paid off in this good grade."

4. Affirm that families are for bragging. Since we can't brag too boldly with other groups for fear of hurting someone who didn't enjoy the same success, we can always come home and brag big. But even within the family we don't compare ourselves to siblings or cause hurt in other ways.

5. In obedience to Romans 12:15, rejoice with your teen when things go well and encourage other family members to do so.

Help Your Teen Develop Relationship Skills

Troubles with friends are big reasons for moodiness in teens. Cliques, slamming with words, hierarchies based on popularity, and kids who can fake their way with adult leaders can cause understandable dismay. Coach your teen and her friends in building a truly good group, one that accepts new people as well as cares for those who are already a part of the group, one that provides a bit of God's kingdom right here on earth (Matthew 6:10).

- *Be friendly.* Smile and greet people happily so they will believe you're glad to see them.
- *Look.* Make eye contact to show you care about each individual.
- *Affirm.* Deliberately compliment people.
- *Speak.* You'll snub by accident if you don't speak to people on purpose. Open your talking circle by inviting those who have just walked up into your conversation and giving them the gist of what you're talking about.
- *Stand strategically.* Put the newcomer between you and your friends so she will be physically in the midst of the conversation rather than on the outskirts.
- *Like yourself.* Assume people want to talk with you and that you're interesting. If you like yourself, others will like you, and you can genuinely like others rather than use them. (See Mark 12:31.)

ACTION STEPS

Don't forget to take time to enjoy your teenager. In so doing you give your teen a strong foundation on which to stand during times of intense emotion. With that foundation, show your teen how to respond kindly to each emotion, whether happy or sad. Point out constructive actions that address each emotion, and help your teen follow through.

What Scripture says: "I, wisdom, dwell together with prudence; I possess knowledge and discretion. To fear the LORD is to hate evil; I hate pride and arrogance, evil behavior and perverse speech" (Proverbs 8:12-13).

Explain to your teen: "Certainly this emotion is intense. But we can choose the wise action and the loving word that solves this emotion no matter how wonderfully or horribly we feel. Emotions are gifts from God, meant to be arrows that direct us, not bosses that control us."

MY TEENAGER CHALLENGES
EVERYTHING I SAY

HANDLE REBELLION WITH LOVING FIRMNESS

Your teenager is challenging everything you say?

Then rejoice!

Why?

You must be doing your job as a parent. And your teenager is doing his job. It's your teenager's job to question what he hears so he can determine what is reliable and what's not. Through questioning he learns discernment and develops convictions. It's your job to know God's truth, to teach that truth to your children, and then to stand firm so your teen will recognize the solidity of that truth and live it boldly in everyday life. If he questions you, he is actually begging you to give him safe places to land.

That doesn't mean it's easy; it just means it's vitally important. When you try to guide your teen in these ways, you'll get eye rolling and verbal accusations, such as "You're so mean" or "You can't possibly be serious!"

These constant challenges can make you start second-guessing yourself. They can make you believe you're being too harsh. They can make you wonder if maybe you're wrong after all. But don't give in to the doubts that your teen's opposition sows in your mind. Instead, translate that worry into an opportunity to pass on God's values. Your teenager won't hug your neck when you insist that she ask before she borrows clothes from her sister (see Philippians 2:4). But you keep on insisting, because you know this will teach her to ask first, rather than just take. This will enable her to live harmoniously not just with her sister but with future roommates.

What If I Really Am Wrong?

You're only human, so on occasion you might miss the mark. It's all right to admit that. Just make certain that your *mea culpa* is based on your really being wrong, not just your teen's insistent challenges. And don't allow one mistake to make you so ashamed that you stop parenting. Look closely, correct any wrongs, and then get back in the saddle. Start by asking yourself:

- Am I actually teaching a biblical principle, or did I find this rule somewhere else?
- Do I want to win for the sake of my teen's character or for my own stubborn pride?
- Have I escalated this to a point where I need to back off, take a deep breath, and start over?
- Am I condemning my teen ("You'll never amount to anything!") rather than actually guiding my teen ("You need to reconsider your decision because it could hold you back from achieving your goals")?
- Am I a dictator rather than a disciple maker?

Ask these questions boldly, but don't stop there. Seek out solutions and then act on them. Every one of us will fail our teenagers in at least some small way. We'll confuse what our teenagers actually need. Or we'll let our own fatigue lead us to neglect our teens or fail to be there when we're needed. Rather than use this as an excuse, though, use it as motivation to minimize your failures and build upon your successes.

All she sees is that you're limiting her freedom.

Do it anyway.

Why? Because when she's looking for her favorite sweater, she'll be glad for the security of knowing it's in her closet rather than on her sister. And when a bigger issue arrives, like deciding who to marry, she'll look for someone who communicates openly and cooperates truthfully. And her home will be happy.

All that from a simple ask-before-you-borrow rule?

Yes. That and more.

Failing to provide steady guidance is like letting your teen fall into a bottomless abyss with no net to catch him. He wants to reach out and find something to grab on to. He doesn't want those handholds to pull loose no matter how hard he tugs on them. He needs them to keep him from plummeting to his destruction. So get ready to be the meanest parent in the world.

You won't actually be cruel—you'll imitate God's method of winning others over through love. You won't be militant—you'll imitate God in the way he stands firm but explains the how and why of his directives. But, like God, you will have to make your rules and your values clear. There will be times when your yes has to mean yes and your no, no—even when your teen protests (see James 5:12). Like God, you'll give security and ever-dependable love.

DELIBERATELY PASS ON GOD'S VALUES

It's easier to stand up to a teenager's constant challenges if you recognize that rebellious teens are actually terrified teens. They have nothing secure to hold on to, and they are crying out for real actions that really work. So be courageous enough and energetic enough to provide handholds for your teenagers. Give your teen the God-designed boundaries he needs to find what works and what doesn't.

Let's say your teen not only challenges you openly, but he also tries to wriggle out of family rules and requirements. You tell him the rule, but he finds some way to get around it. A common situation involves the family car. You told your teenager he couldn't drive the car this afternoon, so he let his friend get behind the wheel and off they went. Your intent was for the car to be there when you got home from work since it was big enough to haul the props you needed for your son's surprise party next week. Now you're stuck with the tiny car, and you don't have time to make extra trips.

If your son had waited for you to get home, he could have used the smaller car. But he didn't know that when he decided to bend the rules. Neither did he know that you were planning to use the larger car to collect items for his surprise party. When he gets home later that evening, how do you handle the situation? Do you cut him some slack since he didn't know you wanted to make preparations for his party? Do you tell a funny story about how he'll grow up to be an escape artist, wriggling his way out of any straitjacket? Or do you get angry and fuss that he could have had a surprise party, but now you're forced to spoil the surprise since he took the car when he was told not to? Any of these responses might seem appropriate, but each one is a big mistake.

Those responses fail to teach your son that crime doesn't pay. Instead, they teach him that the more he sneaks around, the more attention he'll get. Instead of learning that rules are to be obeyed even when he doesn't know the reason behind the rule, he'll conclude that family rules unfairly spoil his freedom. He'll conclude that he can do whatever he wants and that what you say holds no weight. When you don't bother to follow through, he learns to disregard your legitimate rules.

When you fail to connect your teen's actions to the natural consequences that follow, your teenager develops a pattern of ignoring what people say unless it suits him. Later he'll wonder why he can't keep a job, can't get along with his marriage partner, and keeps getting into messes. He already wonders why doing whatever he wants to do and experiencing more freedom don't make him happy. Letting him remain totally self-centered keeps him from letting God be God and from nestling in the security that comes with obedience.

Rather than obey God's directives to not lie, covet, or steal, your son excuses those actions with "I didn't mean to." Rather than choose to love others as he loves himself, your son determines that twisting the circumstances and using people are okay because that gets him what he wants.

It's not true that parents are responsible for their children's spiritual choices. God has no grandkids. But it is true that what a teen experiences in his home profoundly impacts his understanding of God, both

---

MAKE THE MOST OF YOUR MISTAKES

We all make mistakes, so don't compound the problem by allowing your mistakes to keep you from parenting your teens. Instead, practice these remedies:

- If you talk before you listen, stop and hear all the relevant circumstances and then instruct.
- If you declare dictatorially, start fostering dialogue and interaction.
- If you shout, immediately lower your voice.
- If you're afraid you'll do the wrong thing, search out additional resources to show you what to do.
- If you don't know what to do, find a person or resource that can explain to you what is happening and what you should do about it. Your spouse, teachers and coaches, youth workers, the school counselor, and your church's youth pastor can be great resources in times such as this.

---

his love and his authority. Experiences with parents impact the probability that a teen will or won't honor God with his life.

So when you are the parent of a teenager, stand firm. Don't do this by squashing all resistance. Your son's inventiveness (shown through resisting you) and his persistence (shown through getting what he wants) can actually become great character strengths. Redirect instead. With a little redirecting, these qualities can become powerful ways of honoring God and family. This won't happen with wishing and hoping. You must act. Your role is to take your teenager's inborn qualities and channel them into the right avenues. With your guidance:

- Persistence moves from manipulation to commitment to what is good.
- Shyness moves from withdrawal to tenderness.
- Compassion moves from hypersensitivity to expressed care.
- Energy moves from vandalism to fuel for fighting for what's right.
- Intelligence moves from evil intentions to producing a cure for cancer.

STEADILY BUILD CHARACTER

Maybe you think I'm too idealistic, that I could never comprehend what it's like in your house. I can hear you thinking: *You don't understand! My teen's eye-rolling resistance is not just a passing thing. He has a counterpoint for every single comment I make. He can argue the spots off a dog.*

So can my teenagers. Your teen's argumentative stance is no different than that of any other teen in any other family. Not all teens argue with their words, however. Lawrence argues with his actions. If his parents tell him not to go to a certain event, he tells them he's going to a friend's house and then sneaks to the forbidden party. If his parents tell him to do his homework, he says he's finished and then conveniently "remembers" at bedtime that there's this one other assignment he still has to do.

Whether your teen argues with words, actions, or a combination of both, you've got to blow away the smoke screen and get to the heart of the matter: "This is what needs to be done, Lawrence, so this is what *will* be done." And yes, you really can make your teen do what needs to be done (see chapter 4). This could range from the simple complete-your-daily-life tasks to the complex and life-changing choose-friends-and-dates-who-are-Christlike choices.

If parental wisdom really does contribute to a teenager's success in life, why are teens so intent on arguing over everything?

- Their arguments often mean they like what they hear, but they want to know more about the hows and whys. They want to know which handholds will keep them from plummeting. They want to confirm which answers really work.
- Or their arguments could mean that they don't want to be inconvenienced by your rules. They don't want to take the harder path. They prefer the easy option of doing what they want to do when they want to do it.
- Or their arguments might raise legitimate questions because there are a few important points you have failed to consider.
- Or maybe you really are wrong on this one.

Make certain going into it that you have thought things through and that you're enforcing a biblical absolute, not just a personal preference. Then boost your courage to insist that your teen do the right thing with the recognition that a teenager's stubbornness can become the very commitment that makes him rock-solid in the face of pressure to do wrong. This won't happen instantly or automatically. You'll have to actively guide your teens over and over again, year in and year out, to chisel and mold their natural strengths and weaknesses into solid and consistently godly character. But it will happen as you insist on the whats, hows, and whys of Christlikeness.

A word of warning: If you are in fact a fake, your teenagers will know it. Teens watch how you live to see if it squares with what you say. So practice what you teach. Show through your actions how to treat people, how to build friendships, how to work diligently. Your teens still may buck against you, especially when your directive is inconvenient for them, but they'll eventually respect your authenticity.

Solutions for Disrespect

Suppose your teenager has a habit of showing disrespect, and you insist that he speak kindly to each family member and all of his friends. You allow no slams, no put-downs, no gossip. Then he verbally assaults his brother, calling him a wimp and a doofus.

You overhear it, and you call him on it. Later you catch his brother doing the same thing, and you stop him.

After a pattern of such steady intervention, your son discovers that not only will you insist on his treating his brother with honor, but you'll also insist that his brother give him the same treatment. Their relationship will become a good and supportive one, the kind of trusted family relationship that all teenagers crave. With that security, your teen will have much less need to prop up his own self-esteem by denigrating others. And he will experience less of an urge to prove his masculinity away from home through wild behavior or other "manly" pursuits that are anything but manly. Instead, he'll become a Christ-like man.

Your son doesn't realize all this when you call him on slamming his brother. So he complains about the rule. Rather than argue the long-term benefit, you calmly up the consequences—"Lawrence, because you've talked ugly and complained, you can take the garbage out right now."

"But that's Derek's job!"

"It's yours tonight. And if you fuss again, I'll give you another chore."

Following through on what you say gives your words credence, and it gives your son a secure place to land. He'll buck—that's a teenager's job—but as you hold tight, you'll give him a firm foundation, a place where excuses have no power and where family is dependable—and valuable.

As part of your guidance, respect your teenager enough to explain why you ask what you ask. This is not standing up for yourself as much as giving your teen the why and how so he can make his own wise choices the next time:

GIVE REASONS FOR WHAT YOU'RE ASKING

Though teenagers are famous for asking why in order to delay doing what they've been asked to do, they also really want to understand your reasons. Here are effective ways to communicate reasons without being manipulated:

- "Why am I so mean? Because I want you to be easy to live with."
- "Why can't you call in sick? Because it's not true. Also others at work would have to cover for you. You don't like it when they do that to you. So treat them with honor by going on to work when you're on the schedule."
- "Why can't I just do your chores? Because if we split them up, we all have more free time. Now get to it. As soon as you're done you can go meet your friends."
- "Why no alcohol? Because it keeps you from having fun and from making real connections with people. It's no fun to have a party that you can't remember or that makes you sick."

"You can't put Derek down, or anyone else for that matter. Respect—not criticism—is the foundation for good relationships. Derek knows stuff and you know stuff. So respect and value that. Derek has feelings and you have feelings. Respect that. You've both had good times and bad times. Value that. Then treat one another as an irreplaceable person who wants others to cherish his knowledge, feelings, and experiences. To do that, listen to each other, enjoy one another, and laugh together. Why? Because those are the actions that build love. A nice side effect is that Derek will do the same loving act right back to you."

Your teen won't give you a big hug for all this wisdom. He'll probably ask you to stop lecturing him and to quit trying to force him to be so nice. But give him handholds anyway. Brick by brick, you'll build a castle of character that stands strong.

You Won't Have to Fight All the Time

A wonderful side effect to standing firm, even when your teens rebel, is that there will be less fighting in your home. Fights will still come from time to time, but they'll be occasional skirmishes rather than battle-to-the-death wars. You'll be able to talk things through rather than fight them out.

Why?

Your teen knows that you say what you mean and you mean what you say. You've not only treated him with respect, but you respect yourself: "Because I say it needs to be that way, I will act with integrity to make certain that's what happens." This extraordinary dependability gives teenagers a foundation for happiness.

While you and your teen work toward this point of mutual respect, you may have some major confrontations. But in time your home will become a peaceful place where arguments occur occasionally rather than constantly. To get to this place you'll have to act honorably no matter how your teen acts. You'll have to be persistently loving and firm. But the peace that results will be unspeakably precious.

FIVE WAYS TO KEEP THINGS CALM

Neither teenagers nor their parents like the results of a fight—alienation, sadness, regret, and shame. Yet we find it all too easy to be drawn into a fight. No matter how your teen acts, you can avoid this unpleasant path by remembering the word SLICE.

Stop trying to use logic. When you tell your I-don't-have-time-to-eat-in-the-morning teen that she has to eat breakfast before fixing her hair, don't bother repeating that she needs to be well nourished in order to learn at school. She will just argue back. Simply explain the realities: "Why this rule? You spend so much time on your hair that you don't eat. So you can choose to work eating into your schedule, or you will lose beautifying time."

Lower your voice. When your teen argues loudly about what you have just asked, respond quietly rather than try to talk over her.

Implement what you've asked. Subtly stay in the kitchen to be certain she eats well. If she misses the bus, she pays for the gas for you to drive her to school.

Communicate that it's nonnegotiable. "You have to eat breakfast and you have to get to school on time. If you eat well, you can have beautifying time afterward. If you don't eat, no beautifying time. It's nonnegotiable."

Exclaim over successes. Teens quit trying when all they hear are negatives. So pepper your parenting with positives as well as corrections: "You ate well, look great, and you were ready before the bus arrived. Way to manage your morning!"

Invite Your Teen to Say
Anything He Wants

Communicate repeatedly to your teenagers that they can say anything they want as long as they speak with respect. They can disagree. They can tell you about fears. They can share dreams. They can lay their doubts on the table. They can compliment you. But they can't fight or be hateful when they say any of this. You can't either.

Kind and open communication brings closeness. It helps parents know what their teenagers need. In teenagers, it cultivates receptiveness to their parents' guidance. It helps each of you to trust and cherish the other. It promotes family unity.

Am I just dreaming or can there really be closeness between parents and teens?

This is no dream; it's reality. I see it over and over in real families.

Some of the specifics have changed, but the basic needs of life have been the same since Jesus himself was a boy. Teenagers and adults alike need love, security, guidance, understanding, togetherness, and workable strategies for managing life. You remember your own teen years, when you suffered the agony of trying to catch the attention of the one you liked. You know the desperate feeling of failure when you didn't make the team. You remember how important it was to have your hair just right before going out in public. You know the fear of doubting what you've always thought was true. You'll never forget the ecstasy of finally mastering chemistry or trigonometry.

As you remember your feelings and experiences, you won't club your teenager with them. Instead you'll use them as links. You'll fuel trust that you really might have an idea of what could work in that circumstance.

Put Yourself in Your Teen's Shoes

Remember when you were young but wanted to be older? Scared but wanting to be secure? Dreaming but wondering if dreams ever come true? Hoping and not wanting to face disappointment? Lonely but wanting friends? Full of goodness but wondering if anyone cared?

You put up a screen of "everything's fine" and "I don't need any help" so no one would see the muddle of doubts and questions at war within you. How might an adult love you through that, cherishing your dreams while acknowledging your fears, giving you support without making you feel spineless, showing you what to do while letting you learn for yourself?

The answers to this question are the essence of good parenting. Your teen needs both understanding and action. Understanding alone is insufficient for effective parenting. It doesn't solve problems. It doesn't change things. It's just a starting point.

Likewise, action alone won't provide what your teenager really needs. Action alone is dictatorship. Your teen will feel like a puppet with you pulling the strings. Together, action and understanding are the two arms of a much-needed hug. They give your teens the power, security, and love they need to enjoy life.

Say your teen feels superstressed. Each of his teachers assumes her class is the only one he takes. They not only give a lot of homework but also assign projects that require library time and the assembly of models. Add to that church responsibilities and a part-time job. Your teen sees no light at the end of the tunnel. Cheating becomes a huge temptation. So does snapping at family members and accusing them of not understanding how rough he has it.

So use the hug of understanding and action to parent your teen through this tough time. Understand first with words like, "Lawrence,

I still remember the agony of my junior year of high school. And that was back when we didn't have computers to speed up the process. What do you think will help?"

"I don't know. I just don't think I can do it all."

"What if we come up with some kind of plan?"

"I don't have time for planning right now, Mom. I have to finish Friday's project."

"But planning will save you time in the long run."

"It may have worked for you then, Mom, but you didn't have my teachers!"

Use your parental understanding to realize that your teen does feel pressed, but the plan really will save time over the next several stressed-filled days. Use the other arm of your hug by supplying helpful action: "Why don't you use a day planner? It's a step up from the assignment book you used in middle school. This one allows you to break down your projects into sections and assign the sections to each day."

You insist that your teenager sit down with you and map out his assignments on the planner you provide. Forty-five grueling minutes later, your teen has his projects broken down into manageable segments on his calendar. He fought the process. You feel like a heartless taskmaster. But the job is done. Time will tell if it worked.

The next day he comes home from school, hits the projects on the day planner page, and then relaxes knowing that's all he has to do for the day. It was still a big assignment. The afternoon and evening were still consumed by trips to the library, by writing and rewriting a rough draft, by complaints about unfair teachers. But there's a different tone, a tone of mastery rather than hopelessness. And your teen actually thanks you for the idea.

Not all days will end like this. Very seldom will thanks come this close on the heels of specific guidance. Many times you'll have to try several actions before you find the one that works. But every day, you can add a bit of guidance and a vote of confidence, brush strokes that add excellence to the portrait of your teenager's character.

Keep On Keeping On

You've tried. Really you have. But the monsters that threaten your teenager's happiness and success keep coming. You know that powerful forces conspire every day to prevent your teenager from developing

---

THE POWER OF SINGLE-SENTENCE LECTURES

Speak more than a few sentences in a row, and your teen will accuse you of lecturing. Bypass this by using single-sentence lectures like these:

- The best friends are those who give as much as they take and take as much as they give.
- You only have so much of you to go around, so choose wisely who to spend your time with.
- A little sleep can make a big difference in your perspective (see I Kings 19:3-9).
- Isn't it cool how sticking with the right thing produced such a good outcome?
- I know it's hard, but because we can't change it, we have to persist through it.
- Yes, you have to have a chaperone for that coed camping trip. Want me to go?
- Hold out for the good dates, not the easiest-to-get dates.
- I'd rather have an honest C than an A earned by cheating.

Hint: Try saying at least some of the above through e-mail, notes, and other written communication. Writing it down can make it more palatable.

---

godly character. In fact, you knew them before you ever opened this book:

- lack of communication
- bad friends
- self-centeredness
- irresponsibility
- disobedience
- temptations and destructive patterns
- lack of spiritual connection
- laziness
- unharnessed emotions
- outright rebellion

You have attacked each of these monsters with the hug of understanding coupled with effective action. The problem is that as soon as you shoo away one monster, your teenager rolls his eyes with the firm conviction that you have no clue about him or his life. He makes you feel not only incompetent but also nosey. You've tried the principles in this book. You've stood your ground and been consistent. But your teen insists on arguing with you. He is absolutely convinced that he knows more than you do about a certain subject or event.

So stand firm one more time.

The need to parent well won't be over in one action, a dozen actions, even a dozen years of actions. Your teenager needs to learn to discern between what is true and what is counterfeit. When you persistently live out the truth, his bucking is a compliment to you, to God, and to all parents.

See the God-inspired guidance that you give your teens as a set of bookends. You start by insisting that your teenagers obey what is right and good. Then, between the bookends, add in the ten solid actions described in the chapters of this book. Cap it with the other bookend by affirming your teens for choosing to adopt God-honoring attitudes and actions.

To help you keep at it, take the hand of another parent: your spouse or a committed-to-parenting friend. Insist that your teen obey you, not to fuel your ego, but to fuel your teen's character. See obedience not as unthinking compliance but as a demonstration of trust in you and trust in God. Because you really do know more about how life works, your consistent parenting—even in the face of eye rolling—lets your teen in on the secrets to happiness and joy.

Why go to all this effort? Because the delicious closeness of steady respect will come right on the heels of the eye rolling. You and your irreplaceable teen will discover with absolute certainty that walking through life together is the only secure basis of true family happiness. And your heart will burst with pride when your very real teenager says, "What do you think, Mom? Why do you think God commands this, Dad?"

What just happened? Togetherness happened. And your teen will have learned to transfer his obedience to the only One who always knows exactly the right thing to do—God himself.

ACTION STEPS

Your teenagers need a secure place where people are good, where rules make sense, and where decisions are dependable. So provide that in your home by continuing to parent when your teenagers rebel. Otherwise you'll take away the very foundation they keep jumping on to see if it's secure enough to hold them.

What Scripture says: "Love must be sincere. Hate what is evil; cling to what is good.... Live in harmony with one another" (Romans 12:9,16).

Explain to your teen: "I'm directing you to do this and say this because I love you and because it will help you love others well. I'll love you enough to hold firm no matter how much you buck. Then you can learn to live according to rock-solid values."

WRAP EVERY ACTION IN LOVE

...EVEN WHEN YOU DON'T FEEL LIKE IT

Any dictator can demand obedience. You can force your teenager to comply with the ten guidelines for success that are covered in this book. And there are times that the most loving action is to do exactly that. But don't stop there. Be godly parents who lovingly invest attention in their teenagers with the goal of eventually bringing out heart obedience and true maturity. This loving investment is a daily lifestyle and a persistent mind-set for parents, not a set of come-and-go feelings. Consider each of the ten parenting actions in this book as a love action. Then implement each one with the goal of loving your teenagers like God loves them.

Refuse to assume that your teenagers know you love them. Demonstrate your love every day by guiding and cherishing your teens. As you firmly parent well in the face of put-your-lawyer-to-shame arguments and eye-rolling catch-me-if-you-can challenges, do so with Christlike love. You won't always feel gushy, but you will know deep inside that you're doing the right thing for the right reason.

Choose to act in 1 Corinthians 13 ways and to imitate Jesus. As you love your teens through both actions and words, you'll guide them to act with the same loving actions:

- Show patience.
- Choose kindness.
- Reject bad pride by showing your teenager how to be proud but not prideful.

- Refuse rudeness, and show your teenager how to get along with all people.
- Rather than be self-seeking, seek God's good for all people who will be affected by your anticipated words or actions.
- Keep a leash on your own anger, and show your teen how to harness his or her anger.
- Keep no record of your teen's wrongs by listing them yourself or by telling neighbors about them; address them directly and then move on.
- Refuse to delight in evil, such as treating your teen's misbehavior as cute or funny. Rejoice in truth instead, telling stories about your teenager's good behavior.
- Protect your teen, and show her how to protect herself.
- Trust in the trustworthy, and show your teen how and where to build trust.
- Persevere in good actions and in loving support, because life is hard.

Why so much emphasis on love? Because God is love, because love covers a multitude of sins, because love overcomes fear, and because love leads to a happier life (see 1 Peter 4:8; 1 John 4:18).

The Bible says it best: "If I speak in the tongues of men and of angels [or use the best parenting strategies in the world], but have not love, I am only a resounding gong or a clanging cymbal [or a lecture machine]. If I have the gift of prophecy and can fathom all mysteries and all knowledge [and genuinely know what's best for my teenager], and if I have a faith that can move mountains, but have not love, I am nothing [and I'll be totally ineffective as a parent]. If I give all I possess to the poor [or my teenager] and surrender my body to the flames [or my teenager], but have not love, I gain nothing [nor does my teenager]" (1 Corinthians 13:1-3).

ABOUT THE AUTHOR

Karen Dockrey is a Christian, an educator, a youth minister, a trained theologian, and, most important, a parent of teenagers. She received her Master of Divinity from Southern Baptist Theological Seminary and has been working with and writing for youth and their parents for more than twenty-eight years. She has authored over thirty books, including the *Youth Worker's Guide to Creative Bible Study*, *When a Hug Won't Fix the Hurt*, and the *Student Bible Dictionary*. Karen currently spends her time working with the youth at First Baptist Church Downtown in Nashville, Tennessee, writing for youth and their leaders, and leading workshops across the country on creative Bible teaching and parenting.